Fame

FAME

Susan
Margolis

SAN FRANCISCO BOOK COMPANY, INC.

San Francisco 1977

Library of Congress Cataloging in Publication Data

Margolis, Susan, 1941–
    Fame.

    1. Fame.   I.   Title.
BJ1470.5.M37   301.1   77–12
ISBN 0–913374–70–9

Printed in the United States of America

10 9 8 7 6 5 4 3 2 1

To my father and to the memory of my mother

CONTENTS

Illustration section follows page 102.

Preface

Whenever a famous person walks into a lobby or a theater or a restaurant or a living room, my memory of that room becomes dominated by the famous presence. Why, I've always wondered, should I respond to heroes and to Kennedys and movie stars and Nobel Prize winners and criminals in the same way? What is fame? Is it different from simply being a celebrity? Does a life change substantially when a person is known and stared at and wondered about by more people than he or she can ever meet? What effect does fame have on private life? On death? On patience? On the ability to love? On the public?

It is hard for full-time members of the audience to keep track of what is human and what is image. Many of us are curious about that blur or glow—fame's nimbus—that recognizability that separates a celebrity from the rest of us. When people suddenly begin to treat a person with a new combination of awe and contempt, when everyone seems to want something, even if it's just proximity to the famous person, how does it make that person feel? What changes does it cause? Once famous, how does a person feel toward the people who pull at the clothes and grab the glasses? Gratitude? Contempt? Exasperation that someone on the payroll is deliberately planting teasers in columns and ads in newspapers to make the public want to touch him?

Can we in the audience learn the truth about people who are famous—whatever pride they might feel, whatever guilt they might harbor, however they straddle the line between myth and human being, power and vulnerability? Or is it none of our business? Does the famous human being have the right to total privacy? Is it our right to know who a person *really* is just because his or her image travels into our homes? And what are those images doing to us?

This book springs from such questions and from talks with the famous and with their agents, psychiatrists, staffs, and entourages, most of whom were enormously generous. Many of their names and insights appear in this book; others insisted on talking off the record. I am grateful to all of them and to the following people as well, for information and encouragement: Cleveland Amory, Patricia Burstein, Larry Becker, Peter Bonventre, Rasa Bono, John Brademus, Marie Brenner, Barry Brown, John Cafferata, Sampson deBrier, Marshall Efron, Kenneth Greenblatt, Peter Hackes, Judith Hilsinger, Fritz Holt, Patricia Holt, Helga Howie, Susan Laidman, Harvey P. Laidman, Arthur Laurents, Eric Lax, Esther Margolis, Elaine Markson, Maureen Orth, Joslyn Pine, Paul Rosenfield, Shelly Schreiber, Peter Simon, Peter Tauber, Marlene Van Meter, Mary-Lou Weisman, Max Whitehouse, Richard Winter, Tom Wolfe.

New York   S.M.
May 1977

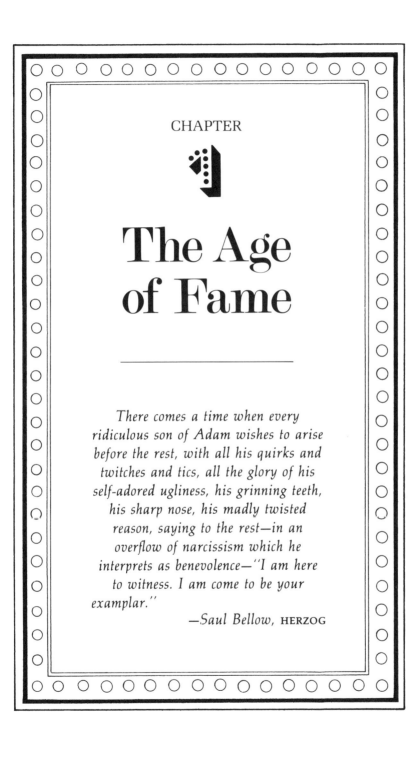

CHAPTER

The Age of Fame

There comes a time when every ridiculous son of Adam wishes to arise before the rest, with all his quirks and twitches and tics, all the glory of his self-adored ugliness, his grinning teeth, his sharp nose, his madly twisted reason, saying to the rest—in an overflow of narcissism which he interprets as benevolence—"I am here to witness. I am come to be your examplar."
—Saul Bellow, HERZOG

Today the gifted as well as the deranged among us are struggling to be famous the way earlier Americans struggled to be saved. Not only musicians, actors, athletes—performers in the old sense of the word—but also poets, politicians, scientists, designers, and assassins are spending at least as much time and energy making themselves visible as they are doing their jobs.

Fame once promised honor and glory and immortality, but in this media age, fame has dissolved into a new slickness and is now indistinguishable from the simple notion of "celebrity." So a good working definition of fame is Daniel Boorstin's "being well-known for being well-known." But fame is richer than discreet well-knownness. Fame still carries with it an excitement, a promise, a sense of holiness or blessedness which is lost when we try to reduce it to simple celebrity status. Fame is an achievement that is acknowledged when more people have heard of a particular person than he or she can ever meet. An award. A reputation. A place in history. A denial of death.

Once fame lust gets into the blood, it can distract the quester from anything else in the world. For some, it is an obsession that results from the urge for revenge, the need to

3

repay adolescent cliques who ignored them; for others it's a compensation for parents who never paid them enough attention. Or it can be a way of avoiding who we really are, a way of playing a role so we never have to look in the mirror at ourselves. There are many ways of explaining it; but the very magic of fame lies in its elusiveness.

Even among the most famous people in the world, almost no one admits to being famous, and even fewer admit to enjoying fame. Part of the hesitation is the egalitarian American impulse; part of it is the ancient taboo of *hubris:* if we admit we have it made, we're bound to fall.

Still, the fame game is the American tournament of the 70s—stylistic and political and religious and athletic:

Stylistic in the sense that it reveals itself with image and image worship.
Political in the sense that it demonstrates the tensions between people of more and less power, and preserves the fetishes of democracy.
Religious in the sense that it provides substitutes for royalty or saints or aristocracy, with rituals and rules as elaborate and exacting as most churches.
Athletic in the sense that it is competitive and has its own rules and goals and players, positions and prizes and arenas.

Fame is a particularly American phenomenon. It is both a feeling and an industry unto itself, continually fed, groomed, and exploited by highly successful newspapers, magazines, and television programs. Fame is the big American product, the closest we can come to making our dreams come true. It combines the religious mystery of immortality, the mythic quest for love, the alien's dream of acceptance, the narcissist's chance for exposure. So the fantasy of fame is more seductive today than the fantasy of sex (which has lost its mystery), or of money (which we no longer believe buys happiness), or of power (which seems to corrupt absolutely).

4

Fame cuts across the textures of morality to include heroes and villains, winners and losers, established celebrities and previous unknowns. Once in the headlines, a Charles Manson or a Jimmy Carter, a Patty Hearst or a John Dean, a Squeaky Fromm or a David Frost, can compel our attention for a moment or a lifetime: these people make news, they are celebrated and so they are famous. And once famous, they invade our thoughts and our conversations in a way that diminishes the significance of their acts and emphasizes *only* the attention, the headlines, the exposure, the appearance—the fame itself.

Fame, then, may or may not incorporate substance: was there a difference between all of the commotion surrounding Elizabeth Ray and all of the commotion surrounding Watergate? No, in fame's terms, it was not the substance of either news event that counted, it was the *commotion*. And fame may indicate more about the whim and mood of an audience than about the virtues or gifts of celebrities themselves: was Anita Bryant the most knowledgeable anti-gay spokesperson to launch the "save our children" campaign? No, it was her fame as the celebrated Florida orange juice promoter that somehow (perhaps because it was so incongruous) struck an exposed nerve of millions of Americans, who responded with intense fascination.

If fame seems to cross the boundaries of substance and morality, it defines itself through a system of categories all its own. There is *face fame* (Elizabeth Taylor, Harry Reasoner), *name fame* (a Rockefeller or a Kennedy), *job fame* (Geneen of ITT), *fame by association* (escort of Jacqueline Onassis, hairdresser of Marisa Berenson). There is *fame by resemblance* (*Esquire* ran a look-alike cover feature which no one praised but everyone read); *fame by disaster* (she lost her hand at the LaGuardia Airport bombing, his child was on the kidnapped bus in Chowchilla); *fame by ideas* (most intellectuals get no points unless, like Norman Mailer, Truman Capote, or Lillian Hellman, they get television speaking

5

time); *fame by familiarity* (Walter Cronkite, according to one poll, could be elected President by a landslide); and, of course, *fame by entertainment* (Bob Hope, Robert Redford, Barbra Streisand). Occasionally one gets *fame by heroism* (Nader, Salk, Woodward and Bernstein), but it is less accessible than *fame by notoriety* (Charles Manson, Sara Jane Moore, Cinque, Sirhan Sirhan).

But the real fun starts when fame players use their achievements in one category to promote new achievements in another category. Redford, Fonda, Beatty, and MacLaine bring their entertainment fame into politics to promote a candidate or a cause. Or Cary Grant, Polly Bergen (entertainment fame), and Diane von Furstenberg (name fame) promote cosmetics or clothes. Andy Warhol moves from art world fame to media-gadfly fame and obliterates questions of quality about his particular form of avante-guardism: because he is a famous artist, his image is greater than his accomplishment.

Charles Manson is said to be recording phonograph records from his prison cell.

Just about everyone who has ever done anything of interest to anybody has written a book about it and then flung himself into the small-time fame circuit of talk shows and newspaper interviews.

And Muhammed Ali took politics (draft refusal), religion (Muslim), sports (boxing), and personal flair (reading his poetry at a press conference or on Johnny Carson) and not only established his image as "The Greatest" but starred in his own movie as well!

But these are all *coups de fame*—juggling of categories and positions and media events for double and triple prizes by the already famous who compete with each other in the higher stratas of the fame game. Underneath, the competition to become famous in any category—and therefore to displace those who are already established there—is fierce. So every professionally famous person hires a go-between to

6

stand between himself and his public for the purpose of image maintenance. For informally famous people, the journalist or the newscaster who interprets what they say is sufficient. A bit higher up, there is the promoter who works for the boss and keeps an eye on the individual athlete or aide. Then there are those people whose particular brand of success depends on little else than the way they appear. They need a personal press agent who censors their words and who plants stories about them in popular magazines. Finally, there's the higher-grade publicist who handles only projects—films or restaurants or shopping malls or charities—and treats them like people he wants to make famous, staging "happenings," and inviting famous people to them so that they may adorn the event the way jewelry adorns the star.

Even higher up there are also people who scoff at personal publicity—the muscle famous—and who hide behind their organizations. They manipulate public opinion by hiring huge public relations firms to influence the famous people who influence the public. Since much of this fame manipulation is among people who prefer power to fame, the general public doesn't know about it and mistakes the stars—the people who prefer fame and fame-power to real power—for the people making the decisions. So newscasters are often mistaken for opinion makers; and when they are, the public relations staff has done its job well. Television networks not only hire entire agencies devoted to public relations, but also employ staffs of at least fifty in-house people who do nothing else.

Fame's prime movers are the opinion-makers, people who are instrumental in contributing to the image of the famous. These are not professional PR agents or publicists, but people who have access to high places and serve as go-betweens between people with clout as well as between the famous and the public. It doesn't matter, for example, if a book about bee-keeping has a laudatory quote on its jacket from Norman Mailer—he is a famous opinion-maker and his name sells copies, even if he knows nothing about the content of the millions of books he helps sell.

There are, of course, professional opinion-makers, ranging from political columnists (Reston, Evans and Novak, Anderson) to gossip columnists (Earl Wilson, "Ear," and Liz Smith) to editorial writers, advisers to the lovelorn, society columnists, and satirists, critics, and reviewers. Most of the time these people are not famous themselves but are intermediaries between the person or product wanting to be famous and the public that can make it, him, or her famous. So columnists, unlike news reporters, broadcasters, or feature writers, have a particular kind of power to turn an obscure notion or person into a famous property; they seem to have an *in* to higher places and are able to translate what goes on behind the scenes into what is most acceptable—or controversial, or trendy, or hot—to the general public. But their role in the fame game is not so much the presentation of information as it is the trading of secrets.

It is important to see the symbiotic relationship between secrecy and fame. Secrecy is what is inaccessible, invisible; but someone has to call attention to it for the audience to realize there is something we don't know. Secretmongers are like snobbish hostesses who don't invite the press to their parties: being excluded creates interest; secrecy becomes in and of itself reason to be concerned.

Of course in many cases, the mystique that surrounds the secret is much more interesting than the secrets themselves. For example, the interest in Elizabeth Ray, or the *real* Patty Hearst, or Nixon's 18½ minutes of blank tape, or Eagleton's breakdown, was far more intriguing than the actual truth behind that interest. In the same way, a reporter may feel tremendous anticipation before interviewing a famous person, then a tremendous let-down upon finding that famous person to be as dull and flawed as the rest of us. Or a viewer watching a talk show may wonder how candid a superstar truly is—but if that star were totally candid, would he tell us what we want to know, would he satisfy our curiosity? Or is our need simply to be titillated rather than informed—that is, do we *want* secrecy, not information?

If the idea of secrecy helps to promote fame, then the trading of secrets becomes an art in itself, communicated to us through a vehicle called gossip. Gossip is both a cause and effect of fame: if the right people gossip about an unknown, others in the right circles will begin to look upon that unknown as an up-and-comer, someone to be watched and, possibly, interviewed or written about; if the gossip is about a famous person, it is simply more grist for the fame mill. It doesn't matter if gossip is complimentary or nasty, so long as it brings a name or face or relationship in front of the public. Thus gossip is produced by the famous, consumed by the obscure, and merchandised by the press.

Since fame has become superficial and transitory and slick and insubstantial, gossip seems to penetrate behind fame's guise to give us a peek at the private, the secret, the exclusive, the real. For gossip exploits the ambivalence of fame's audience: awe and contempt; it lets the famous remain admired (because they are famous) but it also pulls them down off their pedestals to the level of everyday interaction of the rest of us. A quirk, a hope, an eccentricity, a fetish, a fear, a vulnerability in the private life of a public figure provides the secret that, when gossiped about, helps to sell copies or tickets or newspapers or books or tee-shirts. Elizabeth Taylor's seven husbands, Marilyn Monore's miscarriage, Judy Garland's breakdowns, even Totie Field's amputated leg become the very tools of fame, creating in the minds of the audience a more personal involvement with the famous than the quality of their professional achievements could ever evoke. It is as if an unwritten rule to being famous is that once you've made it, "your public" wants it all—they want to see if your public image can be authenticated by your private life. So the more you hold back, leaking out the

9

secrets one by one to the insatiable crowds, the more they'll give you attention and keep you famous. So secrets, rumors, gossip, anecdotes, and tips are the standard devices of the professional publicist whose job it is to keep the fame-consumers talking.

Fame used to mean, simply, reputation, and on the most personal level it still means approval. In the family circle or neighborhood or village, it became acknowledgement or attention. Being the first on the block to do or acquire something, the toughest guy, the glamour puss, the millionaire, are all straightforward, well-defined positions of status, around which gossip is also simple and direct. But now that the global village has replaced the neighborhood, a new television reality has intervened to open up the channels of recognition in enormous proportions, mixing up the quests for love and recognition and heroism and immortality within one single arena: fame.

Television demands our attention and gives intense authenticity to the people it shows us for the moment they appear, and so we make room in our lives and our homes for the diplomat, the actress, the assassin, and the writer as if they were right in our neighborhood (electronically they are) and as accessible as the greengrocer or hairdresser down the street (in reality they are not). Through television we seem to get first-hand gossip and to give approval over the air, not because we are responding to older, more traditional values of wealth, prestige, or excellence, but because television says so, shows so, insists so for that moment and then breaks for a commercial while we sit there thinking about it. Our own rumors seem petty by comparison, and even what we read in the newspaper or *People* or *Us* is less than believable until we've seen it validated on television news shows or talk shows. It is no wonder, then, that fame has come of age in a *television* age: for fame, like television, gives us image without substance; closeups and inaccessibility at the same time.

If notions of honesty, hard work, conviction, integrity, principle, dignity, morality, and courage all become cloudy when observed in the unique arena of fame, then so, too, are the rules for being and becoming famous clouded by the sheer fact of public exposure. It's as if everyone knows what the rules of fame are but no one, if pressed, could ever quite articulate them or write them down.

When Barbra Streisand accepted an Academy Award for her role in "Funny Girl" she reached the podium in such a state of excitement that she babbled an incoherent, rambling description of her childhood desires to be a movie star. Columnists criticized her the next day for being melodramatic and mushy, but actually they were accusing her of what everyone who had seen the spectacle knew intuitively: Streisand had broken the rules; she had let her emotions get in the way, had blurted out a private memory that could have been—should have been—strategically presented in another context, and had embarrassed everyone by gushing and indulging herself in a fame moment.

On the other hand, when Louise Fletcher accepted an Academy Award for her role in "One Flew Over The Cuckoo's Nest," she moved millions to tears by giving special thanks to her deaf parents in sign language while choking up with tears herself. It was probably as honest, gracious, and innocent a moment as we would ever see on the Academy Awards, but of course in the fame game authenticity is irrelevant. What is important—and everyone who watched the Awards that night knew it—was that Louise Fletcher played by the rules: she was not overly emotional, did not indulge herself in instant fame, and did not embarrass anyone; instead she risked just a bit of her private feelings (so we got the peek) to bring a touching moment of gratitude into the fame arena.

Similarly, when Jimmy Carter and Walter Cronkite tap into America's telephone lines, they offer a "randomly" selected number of their countrymen a chance to join them in a fame instant that is broadcast straight into history.

11

Carter's populist image may remain as separate from his personal or even his political philosophy as Cronkite's, but his image has immense appeal and America is touched by his taking the trouble to show it. Honest or not, symbolic or not, straightforward or not, this is, in fame's terminology, good strategy.

Although unwritten, then, there *are* some rules to the fame game by which the players conduct themselves. Obviously it is crucial to have a public image that looks good to the audience, that remains bright and attractive and interesting—sometimes carefully daring—and that always seems to be involved in something new and trendy and fashionable. Some famous people do not have to work very hard at keeping their image polished and shining. These few chosen have what fame merchants call "magic" (Liza Minnelli, Jacqueline Kennedy, Frank Sinatra, Muhammed Ali, Katharine Hepburn, Humphrey Bogart, John Kennedy, Marlon Brando, and the Beatles), and they seem to interest us no matter where they go or what they do. The others (most politicians, writers, and sports stars), however, must fill in with technique what they lack in magic to convince us that what they do is interesting enough to compel our attention. In all cases it is not what they do that is important, actually, but how they carry it off and to what degree it keeps their image famous. In the fame age, substance is not as important as image; achievement has nothing to do with attracting attention.

It is important for famous people to go places where their fans as well as their competitors see them and acknowledge their fame. Usually that clustering takes place on an exclusive as well as public level and with people of the same caliber of fame. Gossip columnist Joyce Haber coined the term for superfamous social gatherings in Hollywood "A" parties.

What makes an "A" party is not so much who is invited but who is excluded. In New York, Elaine's restaurant is an

12

important clustering place for fame-seekers because it's often very difficult to get a table there unless you're officially recognized. Sometimes it is even impossible for the officially famous. Elaine Kaufman is nobody's fool.

In Washington D.C., where exclusivity is most formal, fame plays on the insecurities of the people who are temporarily let in and attracts those who have not yet won recognition as insiders. It's great for the business of the restaurants or for the popularity of hostesses and their parties to know just how much exclusivity they can get away with. Such a system of snobbery of course is not new. But what *is* new is that fame in and of itself—simply being known for being known—gives cachet. Not just in your town or neighborhood, as in the pre-television days, not just in your field of work or personal endeavor, but everywhere—in the homes of strangers, in restaurants and office buildings, in Congressional back rooms and movie studios and "A" parties and conventions. In the fame age, entrance—being able to get in and knowing how to go in—is essential.

The payoff for fame in Hollywood is the feeling that you have star quality and are worth looking at, that all you've got to do is stand there and be photographed, and people will thank you. In New York, where trend fame is king, hipness—being in on the latest moneymaker, scene, fashion, or theater—brings points. The emotional payoff is for being smart, perceptive and First. Not so much the beautiful child as in Hollywood, but the precocious child.

In sports, of course, the emotional payoff is for being tough, brave, strong, and for winning. The competition is intense because the strength necessary to keep up the fame diminishes each year; an athlete's prime is only temporary. Caught like Sisyphus, sports figures throw every conscious spark into their act. And although some of us scoff at the high seriousness devoted to sports, nobody can claim they're not vital to America.

In Washington the reward is epitomized by the public's

surrender of power. One politician who used to be on Capitol Hill explains that all the public glory, all the votes, all the thanks or terror that come as input are important only as a sign that one does a good job. "That's what gets me up in the morning, the fact that I know I do my job well; I need votes to keep on working, and public acclaim is indication that there are more votes out there."

And yet for all the puffery and trumped-up importance of the famous, their competition for attention, their exclusive parties, and their packaged images, the main rule of behavior is to present a seeming effortlessness about it all. Celebrities can arrive at a premier or talk to Johnny Carson or deliver a campaign speech just as easily and smoothly as if they were chatting with just anybody—you and me—across the back fence. This is why famous people work very hard to appear to be slightly bewildered by all the attention, all the press coverage, all the crowds. If they didn't, if they seemed to be basking in it or afraid of it, they wouldn't be worthy of our attention: we would call them arrogant on the one hand or weak on the other. Effortlessness smooths all of that over, providing a slick, chic sheen that allows them to be witty or seemingly candid at just the right times. And it allows us to feel close to them without worrying about human frailties: petty facts, such as body odor or ulcers, would soil the image and diminish the fame.

Another important fame skill is to keep the public image so up-front that private life remains secluded, thereby making the notion of celebrity twice as interesting as it really is. To this end, add strategy and timing: when to leak that special item, when to appear on this or that program, when to run for election or appear to be taking a stand or do that next movie or book or play or dance. Such decisions must be considered at every moment of every day, and the tension that exists between wanting to enjoy fame and getting it in the first place can be explosive. So agents, publicists, psychiatrists, dress designers, beauticians, business managers, and other advisers are called in to weigh the *usefulness* of every act, from shopping at the supermarket to getting married or divorced to undergoing a face lift.

So there really *is* no effortlessness, only hard work and planning, and that's what fame is for people who are famous—it's giving up the romance for the work. But because getting fame seems as simple and innocent as being "discovered" at Schwab's drug store, and since the fun and enjoyment and recognition of fame seem so effortless, many of us in the audience want it, too.

Indeed, fame as we celebrate it in America is democracy pushed to the absurd. What many of us want is what Andy Warhol promised: our fifteen minutes of fame. But for the time being, most of our performances are limited to an audience made up of a few dozen friends or neighbors. While we're waiting to become public figures, we're just folks. Or so we would have it seem. Along the way we discover exactly how our voices sound on tape and exactly how we look when assuming famous poses in the mirror. Media heroes and heroines fly in an out of our dreams whether we like it or not, competing with us, usurping our fantasies. Even recluses polish their images so they can be *real*. Naturally we cannot all become famous—what happens instead is that we all participate in the fame game: we become performers and audience at once.

At a sneak preview of the movie "New York, New York" in San Francisco, when a mechanical failure stopped the film abruptly, the people in the audience, many of whom had waited in line for three hours to get in, hooted and stamped their feet in impatience. Suddenly, a commotion in the back of the packed theater caused everyone to turn around and take notice—there in the back row sat the film's star, Liza Minnelli, who had quietly been sneaked in just before the showing to observe the group's reaction. In moments, the entire audience crowded into the aisles near her and stood there, applauding hysterically, until finally the lights

15

dimmed again and the ushers moved people back to their seats. The film resumed, but something very significant happened, as Joseph Torchia reported the next day in the *San Francisco Chronicle:*

> For as soon as Liza reappeared on the screen, everybody cheered wildly. Everytime she belted out a song people whistled or hooted. When Robert De Niro treated her badly they booooooooed. When she finally launched into a dance step they lost control.
>
> It was as if they were performing for her—letting her know again and again how much they loved her.
>
> "I've always dreamed of that happening," said one man. "I've always dreamed of going to a movie and finding the star sitting next to me, offering me some popcorn, just enjoying watching themselves as if they're somebody else!"
>
> "It was like going to a play," said somebody else. "What a great feeling to know they can hear you!"
>
> "If you ask me it's a big ego trip," said one woman. "It's like looking in a mirror and applauding yourself. It sounds kind of phony to me."
>
> One man asked, "I wonder if she liked us as much as we liked her?"

The star came to the theater to watch the audience watch her perform for them on film, but then the audience spotted the star in person and performed for her as they watched her perform for them. Although Liza Minnelli had left the theater long before the film ended, the audience kept right on performing, giving the movie a standing ovation long after it ended. It was a rare and exhilarating fame moment for everyone, and that moment will live on in the memories of those people in the audience, making them feel closer to her and she somehow closer to them.

The fame game claims us all as participants. As Studs Terkel points out:

16

For the anonymous millions . . . there is a surrogate life to be daily lived. It makes the day go faster for Teddy, the doorman, who watches human traffic at a Loop office building. "Hey," there's a fever to his usual monotone, "who was that just come in? I seen that face, I know. He's supposed to be somebody famous." It matters little whether the face, probably one that has appeared on a TV talk, represents a commercial, a political idea, an art, a science or a call house—for Teddy it is enough. Two, three such winners a week and he has it made.

Others, less fortunate, must make do with images on the TV screen. On rare occasions, when the image in some occult manner materializes on the street, at the airport or in some lucky somebody's cab, the anonymous one experiences the shock of recognition. If the face is Bill Russell's or, God willing, Charlton Heston's, it may provide conversation for an otherwise lost weekend. In any event, it helps the faceless face survive the day.

And while "the faceless" are aware of famous people constantly appearing before them in many different modes and styles—electronically or in print or in person or on screen—it's easy to confuse time and place, image and reality, life and death. And that's the point to fame: to live on in the hearts and minds of the public long after you've retired or passed away; to appear and reappear before them in a constant procession of images that make you no less than immortal.

At Keele University in England, two researchers drew up a list of 71 public figures and asked 114 students to indicate whether each person on the list was alive or dead. According to *Psychology Today,* "the students were wrong more often about dead people than live ones. For example, the less famous a person, the more often he or she was considered dead. . . . Among the better-known deceased, Nikita

17

Khrushchev, Margaret Rutherford, Humphrey Bogart, and July Garland all had many admirers who thought they were still alive."

Indeed, the likes of Bogart or Garland *are* still alive in much the same way they were alive thirty years ago: through their images, their performances, their stardom, their fame. Thus "the confusion about Rutherford, Garland and Bogart is understandable," wrote *Psychology Today,* "because their films are still shown regularly on television." Of course, if it ever happened that such films became passé and were not shown over and over again on television, this kind of fame would die with the next passing generation.

For those who want to go beyond mere celebrity, who want to be remembered longer than a few generations or a telegenic instant, mythic fame is the ultimate goal. As Heraclitus wrote, "The best seek one thing above all others: eternal fame. . . . One man is worth more than ten thousand, if he is great." But that greatness may or may not exist in the form of real achievement so long as the *image* of greatness is carefully and continuously passed on.

Two years after George Washington died, Parson Weems wrote a book about him that became a best-seller. The book emphasized Washington's Christian virtues, went through twenty-nine editions, and was adopted as a text for school children. It was the source of the "I cannot tell a lie" legend and the symbol of the cherry tree, which invoked the image of a man who never lied, who was strong enough to sling a dollar over the Potomac. Although he was a human being, we remember George Washington as an image, a mosaic of symbols, a figure to be reacted to and reinterpreted by every generation.

In one of his letters, Weems, a book salesman who travelled widely and constantly, outlined the theme of his best-seller:

I show that his unparalleled rise and elevation were due to his great Virtues

18

1   his Veneration for the Duty [sic] or Religious Princi-
    ples
2   his patriotism
3   his magninmity [sic]
4   his Industry
5   his temperance and sobriety
6   his Justice &c. &c. Thus I hold up his great Virtues . . .
    to the initiation of our Youth.

Myth-making is the fame game of history. It differs from
and is greater than the actual events that created it, because
it feeds the common aspirations of future generations and is
enhanced by them as well. Myth is also greater than, as well
as a product of, fame itself. In classical mythology, the
goddess Fama is variously described as the personification
of Rumor, daughter of Hope, partner of Omen, or negatively,
the representation of evil reputation and the opposite of
Glory. Fama was a messenger of Zeus, spreading fame
wherever she went, and associated with the idea of divine
origin. So fame, then and today, is only a part of the larger
universe of myth.

Fame-age America's myth has been translated into something called the American Dream, the idea that any one of us,
through hard work and dedication, can become rich and
famous in our own lifetime and thus separate ourselves from
the obscure masses. And so we also believe in the individual,
the one person who decides to make the voyage to the New
World, to homestead on the frontier, to build the better
mousetrap, to risk everything, all the comforts of material-
ism, for a new vision. But once the American frontier got
pushed all the way past Hollywood and Burbank, the face of
American individualism changed radically. As the popula-
tion grew, the economy expanded and was transformed.
Individualism, as a direct result, multiplied and incorporated, adding new arenas in which to pursue the American
Dream. The rules became more complicated, so that in order
to reach the pinnacles of fame in many arenas, cooperation

was required from lesser minions who only attended the rites of the game.

Many of us, then, are happy to be knights in the kingdom of fame. Camelot, after all, needed more than King Arthur. It was he who pulled the sword out of the stone, but the magic of Camelot was a group effort—each knight's own best efforts combined with the king's own best efforts—allowing everyone, the king included, to create a whole myth that transcended them all, a whole which, like every myth, was indeed greater than the sum of its parts.

The Camelot myth has influenced us all; it's not just some gauzy tale lost in the misty reaches of a long-forgotten past. It links us with the medieval time when people quested and swooned for the sake of love and glory and immortality. The Camelot image was resurrected by Winston Churchill during World War II to call on the British people to put forth their best efforts, to fight on the beaches, to defend their glory and honor. Society women dodged the death and danger of London during the blitz to drive ambulances, care for the wounded, do their bit. Even today many Britons feel that this was the best time of their lives, when they were called upon to do their best, and when their best was an effort for a greater thing than themselves—their country, or at least, the image of what their country could be.

The same Camelot image was invoked for different reasons during the Kennedy era. The stakes weren't as high, the lines were not so tightly drawn, but Kennedy used the group glory to carry on the tradition as if it mattered just as much. Washington during those years carried an aura within its city limits. People were beating paths to the Capitol to do the dull business of bureaucracy because John Kennedy had convinced them that doing their duty mattered. And the image did not rest with the lower echelon, the minions, but pervaded the best and the brightest, who wanted to work for Bobby then, now for Teddy. And there were the aides: who wanted to participate for one brief, shining moment in

20

Camelot; who were smart enough to let the public know what Camelot was all about; whose very position and judgment let us know that they bought no tinsel; who would never settle for a second-hand romance. The Camelot myth prospered and was marketed: "What do the simple folks do?"

We learned the words to the songs of Camelot and sang them, blending visions of the Kennedys, Richard Burton, King Arthur. We heard the announcement of his death over the radio or the television, and all work ceased. We clustered around our sets to see the instant martyrdom of a president be transformed into a myth. The televised funeral, the killing of Lee Harvey Oswald by Jack Ruby, the passing of the flame to Lyndon Johnson, made us all attendants at the death of our leader. Those of us old enough to remember will always know exactly what we were doing the moment we heard of his death.

Every part of the nation reacted to Kennedy's funeral rites. Indeed, since millions watched, the responses to his death were as individual and varied as the numbers. The government, concerned with orderly transference of power and the appearance of legitimacy before the public, quickly formed the Warren Commission. Political scientists, psychologists, and other academics brought out their tape recorders and recorded everyone's reactions to the event. In fame's terms, the event was unique: it allowed them to advance their own fame through their interpretations of the death, their studying of the public entrails. Lawyers and prosecutors (perhaps innocently, but of course, in the fame game there is no such thing as true innocence) used it to parlay their fame. After all, here was the crime of the century; and the Warren Commission didn't qualify to be the prosecutors or judges of the century. Abraham Zapruder, a Dallas dress manufacturer out for a day with his home movie camera, had recorded the event. Prints were bought by *Life* magazine and seen eventually in every home. Freddie Prinze had his own

21

copy of the film which he screened frequently. Kennedy's fame became mythic, left for each generation to interpret and react to, to adopt as a god or a demigod, a figure to model our conduct on, a touchstone of our values, a basis of comparison for friends and lovers.

The patterns of fame, then, whether instant, or eternal, or mythic, have touched us all—from the time we learned about George Washington, to the time we first tuned into television, to the time we mourned the assassination of Kennedy. These patterns became so ingrained in our daily lives that before we knew it—like the audience performing for Liza Minnelli—we were acting them out in our own lives. So the arena of gossip advanced by the Hedda Hoppers and the Louella Parsons of the forties helped form the market for fame in the seventies; while *Esquire* and *Newsweek* published cover stories on the "new" gossip (a re-emergence of an old trend, they said) the real issue, the real motivating influence behind it all, was fame.

Indeed, if the sixties were a time to get in touch with the self, the seventies have become a time for exposing ourselves. Some do it through game shows, some do it in columns, some through *est,* some on televised revival meetings, some in private fantasy. And some, who are already famous, grant interviews: writers tell how it hurts to write; actors tell how it feels to become someone else; painters brag about their drinking capacity. The media people themselves—up until now snug in the fame slot of the global town crier—have even become celebrities. As Dick Cavett once pointed out, many people are tempted to ask Walter Cronkite for his autograph even as he's interviewing them.

When Narcissus fell in love with his own image in the river, he tried to embrace it, and, in so doing, drowned. For a long time the moral to that myth was a warning against self-interest and self love. But in this fame age, self-exposure and self-consciousness have become causes for esteem, turning us all into actors as well as groupies whether we like it or

22

not. So public narcissism, the fuel for the fame game, allows simultaneous participation and pleasure for performer and audience alike.

To understand how this works, we must understand what fame is, how it affects private life, how it interacts with our ability to make and keep relationships, our expectations, fantasies, work energy, ethics, politics, patience, power, and personal packaging. And if we master the skills of the fame tease and the poses of effortlessness, we can then begin to understand how brutally difficult it is for the famous to maintain their images at all times, at all costs.

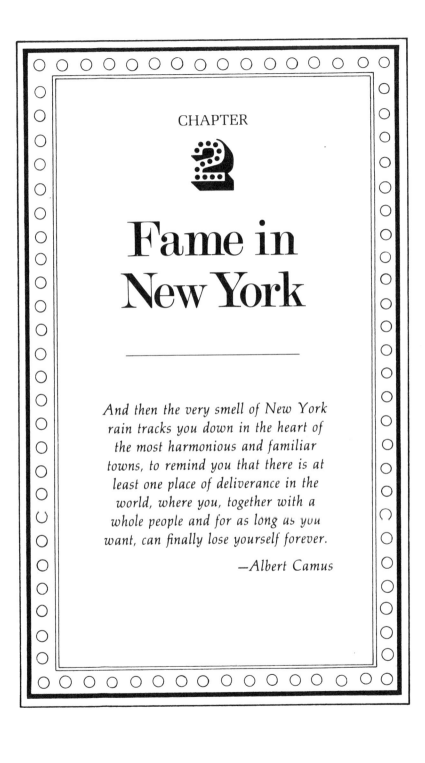

CHAPTER

2

Fame in New York

*And then the very smell of New York
rain tracks you down in the heart of
the most harmonious and familiar
towns, to remind you that there is at
least one place of deliverance in the
world, where you, together with a
whole people and for as long as you
want, can finally lose yourself forever.*

—Albert Camus

1

Feeding Fame at Elaine's

New York's fame speciality is a splendid blend of hype and achievement. It hoards its fame frenzy with an air of exclusivity and then flaunts it in the face of the public— not every spring as in Los Angeles or every four years as in Washington—but every night, night after night, at restaurants and theaters all over town. So there are two separate but simultaneous fame arenas in New York: the local one, which runs itself like a private club; and the public one, which defines itself by its news coverage in order to be sanctified by the rest of the country.

The first time you step inside the door of Elaine's restaurant in New York you're both alarmed and thrilled, if not because of what you see then because of what you don't see. It is a more ordinary restaurant than you might have expected; and at seven-thirty it is almost empty. The proprietor is nowhere to be seen. There are only a scattered set of diners, all of whom turn to took at who's here as you walk in and then look back at each other or at their glasses of wine. They smile. In this particular case it has been worth the wait: someone extraordinarily famous has shown up. It is that highly celebrated, instantly recognizable couple, Woody Allen and Diane Keaton. Him they recognize right

27

away by his slump, his horn-rimmed glasses, his thin body and thinning hair. Her it took them a moment to recognize, but that's because she's looking at the floor, not at the crowd. Everyone silently agrees they qualify as utterly famous, although if you asked her she'd guffaw and apologize; and he'd say, "Famous? it doesn't mean much—it just gets your glasses ripped off your face when you're not looking"; but here they are at Elaine's—feeding place of New York's fame cluster—and they are not mobbed, not asked for an autograph, not photographed because there are no on-duty *paparazzi* allowed here. They are simply admired and whispered about.

The diners go back tentatively to their salad or their lamb and continue to watch the door with one eye. Customers come and are seated. The place begins to fill. Other celebrities appear, a collage from New York's scores of fame statuspheres: Diane von Furstenberg, producer Barry Diller, Carl Bernstein, Nora Ephron, Lee Radziwill, Andy Warhol, George Plimpton, Howard Cosell.

Elaine herself walks in now looking slightly annoyed, greeting guests as if she knows exactly who they are and can't care less because she has more important things on her mind. She seats herself at the front table near the bar across from the two pay phones so she can keep an ear and an eye on the door and keep waiting those she wants to keep waiting and toss her arms around her favorites, hoping they'll come back tomorrow.

There is no present tense in New York City. Its past is at constant war with its future; and with the self-consciousness of a split personality, it is constantly eating itself up. The moment a New Yorker becomes famous he is set up for replacement, so the fame poses most effective here are those of hurry or indifference. Being late is a sign of being in demand; punctuality is a public sign of insecurity. There's no time for the present. Clocks and watches are essential—not as reminders to be on time so much as indicators that there's some further place you're expected by virtue of your public desirability.

Fame in New York is the appearance of being successful where thousands like you have failed. For the very reason that this is the capital of the thrust against the odds in big business, sports, music, crime, fashion, literature, ideas, and art, the idea of being at the top must always be an illusion. Nobody knows for sure whether the top is at the pinnacle of the World Trade Center or on the front page of *Women's Wear Daily* or in the Felt Forum of Madison Square Garden or at the backgammon table at Elaine's. Nobody knows for sure if Elaine's is as authentic a fame forum now as it was last night because the forums shift as often and as quickly as the players. Hard-edged competition is the New York mode and, unlike the Washington and Los Angeles fame arenas where there's just one major industry in town, nobody outside a given statusphere ever can be sure of a given success story in New York.

So the celebration of fame is a roving ritual—always changing, hard to keep up with; what's famous must be new, must make news, must kill time—all the time before it. And every fame instant will be killed by what goes on next.

The cooperative illusion in New York is that fame flaunters are a new and elite aristocracy. To keep up the air of exclusivity of each celebration, official launchings dispense gold tickets to the general audience and pale silver embossed ones with a gold crest for the creme. Each premicre holds several rows of seats cordoned off for key people and their entourages. Restaurants have good tables and bad tables and tables kept empty for effect. People are treated with varying amounts of deference as they arrive; and being kept waiting is part of the show.

But since there's not enough room for all the people who want to walk around in this city, let alone to occupy the rarefied world of fame winners, even among those who would not call themselves elitists, fame becomes a rationale

29

for exclusion, like country clubs. It is no accident that many
fame clusters choose for their arenas watering holes, feeding
places. Since famous people are groupies too, they bustle
around themselves quite comfortably, possessive of familiar
surroundings, basking in what feels like honor, trading
praise and sympathy, gossip and favors.

To make such exclusivity work, there is almost always a
figure like Elaine Kaufman in such an atmosphere. Call her
the madonna, the bitch-goddess, the earth mother, the stage
mother, the nurturing womb—the fame world needs a hundred such people, ostensibly peripheral, more motherly than
glamorous, hefty but vulnerable, at once soothing and
threatening, waiting to be pleased. So Kaufman feeds drinks
and recognition to the famous and near famous and to fame
voyeurs. Once their fantasies are publicly fed, they can go
back to work. Kaufman has the reputation of being a
powerful shrew, a meanie, a thick-skinned cow, a favorites
player. She knows her reputation and says, "I can't take my
job too personally. I spend fifteen hours a day at this place
trying to make famous people feel good about themselves."
So she produces a show for her patrons in which they are the
stars and the investors as well as the audience. She offers
struggling writers good tables and keeps Henry Ford waiting. She is ostentatiously generous to a few of the obscure,
gambling that they'll give the place the right mystique. She
kicks out Norman Mailer and buys free drinks for an
unknown actor. It works.

Her patrons silently congratulate each other as they arrive. Even though they may belong to any one of a multitude
of different statuspheres, they are partners in fame: an
Italian film director, a Texas novelist, a northwestern congressman, an editor of a national news magazine, a photographer, an investigative reporter. All sit at adjoining
tables, pleased to be together. They taste each other's food,
buy each other drinks, talk movies and clothes and dinner
parties, and tell stories about their day. Some have been
among the chosen first to see a shoe salon open at Bloom-

ingdale's; others come from the first screening of an important French film. Still others, dressed to the teeth, are
enveloped in the aftermath of a gala premiere of a highly
publicized American film.

"Mixed reviews," disdains an eavesdropper who didn't
see it yet. "Let me have another taste of your lamb." The
lamb—all the food, in fact—is adequate but not sensational.
It's as though you're never served enough, as if part of the
service is to keep you hungry. If you never get enough, you
never are satisfied; the anxiety level stays high, and part of
what makes Elaine's exciting is the anxiety that is everywhere. Particularly now that at every table it has been
acknowledged that the famous couple is there. People nod at
Allen-Keaton but no one so far—not even Elaine herself—has
gone up to kiss them. Now their fame has been adjusted to.
They possess the room now. It belongs to them, as if the rest
of the diners have a free chance to glimpse inside their lives
and at the same time sit with them as anonymous equals. It is
a fame instant. People from a dozen of New York's top
statuspheres—society, publishing, fashion, investigative reporting, theater, newsweekly reporting, dance, jewelry, film-
making, art, crime, stockbrokerage—each know that to sit in
a chair at that table with Allen-Keaton could be worth
money and a few hot projects: an important push for the
career of the northwestern congressman; a breakthrough for
the photographer who wants to sell her first screenplay; a
profound scoop for the newsweekly columnist because
Allen-Keaton interviews are rare when they're not pushing a
movie. Many are quite sure their whole life would fall into
place if they could be recognized as famous enough. Some in
the room will lose what fame status they have before the
week is up. Others will be the ones to seize it. Still others will
remain groupies, more comfortable going without a public
sign of hubris. Everyone knows this is their only chance to
meet the famous couple. There is never enough time in this
town. Never enough room.

The next question is: who is the third person with them,

anyway? Is she a relative, a producer, a pending dealer, a new important person nobody recognizes yet?

In this fame instant everyone in the room is equalized in a New York mosaic: they are equals to the extent that they are captured in time, in that tension of watching and being watched, of letting the aura of their local power and potential and prestige be visible off camera and also basking in the auras and the looks of the others present. It is an invigorating moment, particularly because this stranger with the famous couple may very well be on the brink of fame herself, and the co-diners if they're clever, may be the first to figure out who she is, the first to befriend her.

This pressure to be first, to be known and to know, to recognize and to be recognized is a peculiarly New York phenomenon. Perhaps because New York does not have enough time or enough space, the pressure is more painful, the crowds are more dense, the hurry is more desperate. There are so many statuspheres that it is possible to keep track only of the people at the top of each one, never to know precisely how they got there or the exact nature of their achievements. That information is available most exclusively in the form of gossip. In order to be a good gossip, one must know the names and if possible must have met the people behind the names. In New York, name fame is vital.

The restaurant grows more and more crowded. Columnists settle in at the bar. Journalists and movie directors and actors and designers mingle with the socialites and the dentists, whispering at and about each other, kissing each other in greeting, dropping the names of mutual friends. By ten o'clock the place is full and Elaine can be seen playing backgammon with Jules Feiffer at one of the front tables beside the bar, sending after-dinner drinks to selected tables as signs of welcome or congratulations or just to make the chosen ones feel good. Indeed it does feel good to have the waiter lean over discreetly and say that Elaine would like to buy you an after-dinner drink. It might feel even better if

Elaine herself came over, or it might feel like an interruption. So the waiter's ceremony carries a comfortable ambiguity: honor without the burden of intrusion.

There's noise and a frenzied air. Some diners are asked to leave to make room for newcomers. The bar is jammed. People try to give the impression of intimacy. Everyone gets to watch and be watched, and no one can be sure who's worth watching most. At the same time, there's the intense self-consciousness, the reluctance to be seen gawking. There's non-stop murmuring about invitations, where people are off to or in from. Elaine's doesn't mind being a stopping-off place. You are expected to buy dinner if you're not famous, and you may be kept waiting even if you're a regular customer—an agent, say, who brings in customers all the time. In much the same way, a familiar patron may phone and ask Elaine to call Marlon Brando to the phone, and she may choose to say that he's not there, or "For Chrissake, why don't you just leave him be tonight, he's enjoying himself for once." She's also aware of the fact that some people deliberately have themselves called to the phone there.

Insecurity is universal and overwhelming in the New York arena. The race to be chosen is fierce, and the pleasures are momentary. New York fondles its procession of fame winners one at a time and then casts them off to the rest of the country. So millions of dollars are spent every month of the year to help its socialites, painters, designers, writers, architects, doctors, publishers, musicians, composers, philanthropists, dancers, politicians, actors, producers, cartoonists look good.

Looking good means being seen there first, at the right place and at the right time and in the right company, the first to know and be known and the first to walk away, "up" on where and where not to show up, terribly busy, terribly well-dressed, and terribly well-informed. Once famous, those who stay famous manage to slip into an already established

33

fame slot. So Elaine Kaufman is the famous restaurateur in the tradition of Toots Shor. Leonard Bernstein is the musical Wunderkind in the tradition of Stravinsky and Toscanini; Halston is the glamour designer in the tradition of Norell and Mainbocher; Jules Feiffer is the witty cartoonist-playwright in the tradition of Thurber; Andy Warhol is the freak artist in the tradition of Toulouse-Lautrec; Gloria Steinem and Lillian Hellman are the keepers of the public morals in the tradition of Eleanor Roosevelt and Margaret Fritchie. Thus what starts out as transitory and trendy becomes, over the years, constant fame, fed and nurtured by the attentions of those crucial fame-mongerers, the mediacrats.

2

Inventing Media Events

      In New York nobody is immortal. Fame in this city means the simple right to possess the here and now; and that ownership is trumpeted in the media. *People* magazine, the *New York Times*, the network news spectacles, the dinner parties, the openings, and the premieres are the vehicles. The fame drive in the Big City is to capture the consciousness of the public and then to raise that consciousness to include the importance of your achievement. The private hope is that, once noticed, you won't be left out of tomorrow night's fame launchings; you'll be able to keep it up, keep up with the famous and make the Joneses want to keep up with you.

This constant fame ritual promises to transform its achievers from the moment of local recognition—via the mediacracy—to official, national fame. This is because New Yorkers have grown too cynical to share Hollywood's hubris. They know that nothing lasts, that in New York fame is conjured up in instants, not eternity. So evenings at Elaine's carry within them all the dynamics of the local fame arena, but the real thrust of the fame game is national. As the news center of America, New York has the power to make achievement official. Few among the famous or among the mediacrats were born there: most of them are immigrants, and there is a reason why they moved to New York instead of Washington or Los Angeles. New York attracts the prodigies—the ones who are good at being first in their field—and those who like firsts also like trend-mongering the way Washingtonians like secret-mongering. They feed on the anxiety, the crowd, the rush, the desperation, the frenzy: it works for them the way the bacchanals worked for the old tragedians. Whereas frenzy is considered counterproductive in Washington and bad form in Los Angeles, in New York it is the norm. There is a certain pride that comes from surviving the frenzy, and even more pride in profiting from it, controlling it, being visible in it. These are the goals of the local fame game in New York. To be catapulted from your fame slot in the local arena into national fame is the next step.

News, then, emanates from New York the way stardom emanates from Hollywood. It may originate from various places around the world, but New York gives it its official forum. The mediacrats here are both the groupies and the attention getters, so in a sense they have a power similar to that of the moguls in Los Angeles. But most network moguls prefer private power and choose fame fronts like Barbara Walters or Walter Cronkite to be famous for them.

The mediacrats' stand-in power is limited but titillating. Their role looks like a chance to have it both ways: to avoid the risks of glitter fame and the tedium of the groupies, while still having entree to the exclusive realms of the famous. But while the mediacracy looks like a stable fame statusphere, it really offers no more security than being a dress designer or an actor, and perhaps less than being a socialite or plastic surgeon. The fame slot of any newspaper reporter, columnist, or TV broadcaster is easy to fill and refill, like a congressional seat.

So part of the fame tease in New York is the mix of the mediacrats with the stars. Mediacrats are flattered by the fame-by-association: since they attend as many events as the truly famous, they are considered famous themselves. The difference is that the mediacrats serve simply as the fame connection between the achievers and the audience. Their power to attract attention, although it may resemble fame's power, is based strictly on readership, on viewers, on how many customers they can deliver to the sponsor of the party; or on how many will buy tickets to the movie, adjust the hemline, wear the hair-do, assume the pose, imitate the actions of these fame drones who scratch each other's back by helping call attention to the latest trends or gimmicks.

There are various kinds of mediacrats. Of the *paparazzi,* Ron Gallela is the ultimate, the zealous photographer who spends his lifetime haunting the illusive Garbo or the enigmatic Mrs. Onassis, and who spends his fortune on telephoto lenses, or sits for hours in an empty bar waiting for a subject to show up. The *paparazzo* sees himself as part sleuth, part portrait painter. The activities of the famous interest him personally not at all: he is strictly interested in taking the photograph, and his job can mean spending the whole evening covering Jackie Onassis' building on Fifth Avenue (because publicist Bobby Zarem is positive she's going to attend his film premiere and private party in the Grill of the Four Seasons for the launching of a new film) or showing up at the little cocktail party for the former Israeli president whose book is just being launched; or dashing over to a late supper at Elaine's, or to an even later supper at an obscure nightspot around the corner from Jackie's.

While the *paparazzi* are the rather elusive and feisty members of the mediacracy, there are also more recognizable, workaday types: the serious reporters who come to these happenings for news, who treat the launching as an event and dignify it by reporting what opened, who showed up, who wore what and what was served, who said what. Then there are the media gossips who are in it for names. Liz Smith, Earl Wilson, Rosemary Kent—sometimes items are fed to these columnists directly by the publicists, while other times one-liners are written by hired writers (e.g., Woody Allen started out writing gossip items and one-liners). Finally, there are the new journalists who see themselves as students of the manners and morals of the famous.

Tom Wolfe's coverage of the Leonard Bernstein evening for the Black Panthers was the quintessential new journalistic coverage of fame philanthropy. Wolfe covered the event itself and the subsequent press coverage as well. He studied motives, manners, morals, and resisted the temptation to which many of his colleagues succumb—to make his presence the center of the story.

Journalists who *do* write themselves into the story walk the dangerous line between fame fantasy and reality. Every *paparazzo* knows there is no way he can hop into the photograph he shoots, that journalists are simply fame connections. But many mediacrats mistake the intensity of their job for power. Indeed, since the mediacrats who earn their fame by association are paid to live inside the fame romance, their very job is to be seduced by the fame game and to wax eloquent about it. They don't risk exposing themselves by admitting up front that they're in it for fame. They're just doing their democratic jobs: representing the folks back home who weren't lucky enough to be invited.

But most mediacrats are closet groupies who prefer covering famous people to openly seeking fame themselves, and they enjoy the proximity, the favor-trading and the glow. But as they acquire success, they become more and more ambivalent about their jobs unless they're very clear on the difference between themselves and their subjects.

"I discovered Bianca Jagger. I was the first to write about her," claims Rosemary Kent, former darling of the Warhol crowd, founding editor of *Interview* magazine, and a regular contributor to *Harper's Bazaar*. Kent subsequently parted from the Warhol group, but established an independent fame niche of her own when she got married. Although she staged her wedding as a fame event, Kent says she was surprised by the considerable press coverage it received in the *New York Times*. Modestly, she explains that she wanted a cowboy wedding, but

It would have been too expensive to fly everyone home to Texas; so we found this empty building which was big enough to get married in without being too commercial—it was the site of the first Bank of America—and we found six cute Puerto Ricans and dressed them up as cowboys and got a western band from Yale, and we had bride and groom outfits made by the one who does all of Elton John's costumes. And I wore red cowboy boots, and I carried a cactus bouquet with lilies of the valley, and we had six beautiful bridesmaids—cowgirlettes who were dressed in gingham pinafores. And everybody really got off on it: Cherry Vanilla showed up with her bluejean jacket that said "Cherry" on the back, and fishnet hose; and there were Eastside decorators who showed up in salon tuxedos, and Paulette Goddard in her diamonds and rubies, and Diane and Egon von Furstenberg, and my mother wearing a basic mother's dress with little short cowboy boots. I had a friend of mine whose dog flew in from Aspen. People really put out for it, I mean they got up for it.

In retrospect, Kent worries about the conflict of interest presented by her drive to be famous herself. "How much can I write about this world if I'm going to participate in it?" she asks.

It's easy to see how the mediacrats heads get turned by the elaborate shows put on for their benefit, especially since these events are staged *every* evening in New York. Although they resemble the scene at Elaine's, they are by invitation only and require a specific kind of performance. At Elaine's the famous are ostensibly "off duty" and only the columnists are working. But media events are serious business in New York, and everyone works very hard. For the

39

purpose there is to make official the gatherings of various achievers, and to blend the differences between them, to pass on to the public a series of fame instants. Each instant contains a mosaic of people who have nothing in common but their public appearance. And that tableau, that assemblage, also blends the differences between substance and luck and achievement and beauty and lineage and genius, and reduces everyone to a media figure.

Unlike Washington dinner parties where the seating plan is as important as a diplomatic mission, and who says what to whom is the major activity, the crucial element in a New York media event is jockeying not for position but simply for attention. Eyes dart systematically back and forth between reporters and photographers and mirrors and doorways. At these affairs the biggest groupies of all are the ones who are performing.

But few people, whether born into prominence or obscurity, can do the job all by themselves: inventing their own base, catapulting themselves to fame, dressing and celebrating themselves, attending and escorting themselves. Because when the true intentions of a fame-seeker show, he loses the game. And since insecurity is the very food of fame, public figures need help in creating that seductive air of effortlessness, confidence, and elegance that distracts from the tense and desperate business of the show.

So they hire publicists—to arrange and distribute fame bulletins in the form of press releases, invitations to fame launchings, items for the gossips, pictures in the papers. The personal publicist's function is to separate the famous from the non-famous. He censors outgoing messages in the same way a telephone answering service censors incoming calls. This interference creates the impression of such great demand on the fame person, that little time and energy is left for contact with the public. So the publicists create the illusion that it's in the public interest to acknowledge a new trend, that if you're up on this one, you're up there where it counts.

40

Bobby Zarem, champion publicist and mastermind of public premieres, admits, "In the old days of Hollywood premieres, there was really fun to be had; but let's face it, there is no fun at all in being famous now. I'm not even sure there is such a thing as fame—it's all business. Ann-Margret doesn't give a shit about her fans, she doesn't even pretend to."

Zarem has switched from handling one-at-a-time fame names to specializing in entire films or products or restaurants. "The stars get too demanding and it's just not worth it. I broke my back once to get someone a special sound man for a performance at the White House, and she managed to interrupt her nervous breakdown to perform. Instead of thanks, three months later I got a call that the wrong gift had been sent to the President and his wife. I can't handle that stuff. I'd rather orchestrate an entire film promotion than cater to people's emotions."

Perhaps because he is frank about the artificiality of the glamour he creates, Zarem does it with considerable imagination and compelling elegance. Nevertheless, he professes reluctance in giving up his romance about the world of fame. Recently he threw away what he claims was one of the most elaborate collections of autographs in the country. "I'm still the six-year-old kid from Savannah who sneaked away from Sunday School into Tallulah Bankhead's hotel room," he says, clearly proud of the fact that he's still thrilled by seeing in person the very people he works with. When Zarem's father was suffering from cancer and had to visit New York often for chemotherapy treatments, he used to take Bobby along. Every evening he would take his son to a different glamour spot—El Morocco, the Stork Club, Delmonico's—and Zarem attributes his own sense of elegance and excitement to those years before his father died. "But I try to leave all that nostalgia at home when I'm working," Zarem says.

Likewise the people who come to his events are professional about what is expected of them. They know they've been invited for a reason, that their job while they're there is

41

to be seen. Just as Zarem and Paramount may provide them with a free screening and elaborate meal, they are in return providing their own visibility. Their personal payoff is the next day over coffee at the Carlyle, debating with someone who hadn't been invited whether the report in *Women's Wear Daily* is a "hatchet job or a blow job." Being gossiped about in print is the way you know you're established. It's not simply the invitation to a Zarem event that counts but being mentioned in Judy Klemensrud's write-up in the next morning's *Times*. That way you know your publicist is doing his job.

But Zarem manages to do more than his job, or he seems to. He writes longhand invitations and keeps all the celebrities coming back by swearing this next event is not a publicity stunt but a celebration for the people whom he cares about most, the special ones who really *like* being together.

By denying he's in it for fame, Zarem makes the guests feel a gentler affection than is usually offered to them, and in addition they feel innocent again, as if what they're invited to is a chance to be with people who, unlike themselves, are so secure they don't need promotion. It's flattering to think a man so celebrity-bound might really want to take time out for you; and Zarem convinces you he does. So because Zarem makes his gatherings seem truly impulses of the heart, he is as sought after as the people he represents; and scores of celebrities name him as their best friend.

To have a publicist who also "handles" other "desirables" is a godsend. Chances of being invited to media launchings triple when the same publicist handles clients from different statuspheres. So the fashion designer and weightlifter and hairdresser and jewler and socialite and writer-of-the-moment can save themselves the humiliations of having to crash or wangle invitations. If they pay the right publicist enough they'll magically appear in *Newsmakers*, *People*, in Liz Smith's column, in *Eye*. They'll be snapped up for posterity escorting Jacqueline Onassis, glimpsed by a secret source emerging from a limo outside this week's premiere or paged by Elaine for a phone call on a Friday night.

But since the only victory lies in being captured for a moment, the famous are reduced to manifestations of popularity. They are their coverage, their reviews, their photographs, their obituaries. Their experiences become anecdotes; their convictions become slogans. Gossip—both the cause and the effect of New York's blend of popularity and celebrity status—becomes an end in itself; so columnists and reporters are cultivated in shrewd and elaborate ways.

Mediacrat fame is often confused with real power, not only by the journalist but by the fame-seekers who want media access. Maureen Orth says she constantly tries to remind herself that the enthusiasm with which she's invited and greeted around town is addressed to the *Newsweek* after her name. Designers want to dress her, restaurateurs want to feed her; and ambitious men and women from all the local statuspheres want to be seen with her. Her fame connection makes her a handy fame mannequin, more glamorous than many of the figures she writes about.

Barbara Walters, mediacrat and socializer extraordinaire, is constantly asked by her prominent and powerful friends to air an interview with them. It is hard for them to believe that while she has access and air time, she does not have the power to choose whom she interviews.

One millionaire allegedly offered Rex Reed huge sums of money simply to interview his wife. Apparently the mogul doesn't care whether or not Reed publishes the interview. It's just that his wife once told him that her greatest wish was to be interviewed by Rex Reed and he is determined to oblige her.

Gossip columns are considered old-fashioned throwbacks in Los Angeles and Washington; but in New York they are necessary. *Women's Wear Daily* seized on the symbiosis of fashion and gossip and became the champion trend-mongering house organ of the fame industry.

James Brady, who credits himself with putting WWD on

43

the map, in his biography *Super Chic* tells a revisionist fame story so cleverly that one hardly notices how he melds power with fame. The co-stars of the episode are himself, his publication, and Greta Garbo.

> If Greta Garbo were the sort, I suppose she might have considered punching someone connected with WWD during my time at the paper. . . . One day one of the photographers got a tip that Garbo was shopping on East Fifty-Seventh Street. He quickly caught up to her and chased her this way and that as the actress ducked in and out of shops and arcades in a vain attempt to preserve her privacy. Finally she was cornered and the cameraman got his pictures. Back at the office we waited excitedly for the contacts to be developed. . . . When they got to my desk I examined them through my magnifying glass. There she was, that still magnificent face clearly shown in several of the shots. And in one picture you could see how desperately she had tried to shield herself to maintain that legendary privacy. She had held up a newspaper in front of her, between her face and the camera's lens. The paper was that day's WWD.

The passage demonstrates the double-talk that locks mediacrats in with the famous.

Critic Alfred Kazan has explained the constant frenzy of the visible success story simply: "You're never sure of your place." So you keep on doing what famous people do in order to convince yourself of your status.

The prizes of fame are not just the flashbulbs flashing, not the acclaim or the popularity, not the achievement or the titles or the money or the curtain calls. Not even the ultimate obituary. What really keeps all New Yorkers overachieving is the romance they share with the autograph hounds—the groupies' true belief that *famous* means *immortal*.

3

Groupies and Legends

In any media event in New York, the real fame seekers are not the invited guests but those who are excluded, the fans who show up and ask for autographs, pull at sleeves and at pocketbooks. Sometimes they are hired, but surprisingly often they are self-motivated. Like bodyguards and autograph hounds, they orchestrate the fame swell and they happen to love what they're doing. In the news they become simply part of the background, the ones who pay to see what the famous get for free. So publicity is produced ultimately for the pleasure of the nonfamous as well as the famous, the fame pimps as well as the groupies, those who seek fame for romance or entertainment—not for a piece of the action.

Sudden fame can be disorienting, particularly to serious artists who—as most do—spend a good number of years in relative obscurity. A famous face or name that brings the public in too close can foster a paranoia that only gets reinforced by old friends wanting new favors. New York writer and editor Theodore Solotaroff believes that

Writers tend to be discouraged by fame. It's not nearly

45

as delicious as you had thought during all those years when you didn't have any; and it tends to be disorienting because you're not used to your life being taken over by people calling you up for interviews, and being taken out to lunch, invited to parties. And you're not a name for people to ornament themselves with. Either you get with it and incorporate the attention and stay productive, or else you say, hey, this isn't me, and you want to be productive, so you go back to the way you lived before it hit.

Dick Cavett presents himself as an Horatio Alger of fame by virtue of his old-fashioned celebrity worship. "I divide people in two categories: the ones I've actually seen, whose existence I can verify, and the others. I don't have any evidence that Gary Cooper really ever existed because I never laid eyes on him." Cavett's quest for evidence may be what carried his interviewing show as long as it lasted. Chances are that when Cavett became saturated with fame, the groupie in him succumbed and his ratings reflected his loss of interest.

Pure fame exists only in the gazes of passionate courtiers who resemble their cousins the fame-flacks only vaguely. They may be embodied in the autograph seeker who stands for hours at stage doors, airports—everywhere and anywhere a star may appear. But agents, promoters, dressers, drivers, scriptwriters, coaches, gossip columnists, best friends, and even lovers are professional groupies. In fact, many people who are famous themselves are drawn to the famous like moths to a flame, moved and inspired by their prestige, vicariously enjoying their risks and accomplishments, fascinated by their guts and willingness to expose themselves.

Most groupies prefer worship to actual contact. At a recent premiere for a Robert Redford film, a cluster of women outside the theater sobbed in unison like the Eumenides. They had driven all the way from Huntsville,

Alabama, to New York just to see Redford in person; and when they heard the rumor that he wasn't coming, they shook with disappointment.

When a Redford official reassured them their hero would arrive, they waited patiently, noiselessly; and when he finally emerged from his limousine and was mobbed, they were right in there trying to touch him. But they had no particular desire to meet him, to sit down with him and discuss environmental protection. They would never have paid money to go to the benefit for charity, even if they had been invited. Still, their tears were real tears and their fantasies sustain themselves.

Fame is the fabric of capitalism, and capitalist passion needs a sense of mission in order to sustain itself. This is especially apparent in New York, the heartland of big business. And big businessmen by virtue of their power and low profile are more concerned with their personal bottom line than in fame per se. But the famous work for them.

Since the advertising statusphere forms the power core of the fame tease, keeping ahead of the Joneses is the *noblesse oblige* of New York's participants, and they take their jobs seriously—so seriously, in fact, that they make groupies of us all, seducing us to buy the products that famous people buy, or the services, the credit cards, the pet food, the detergent.

How easy, then—and how true—is the assumption that if we'll buy products or services hyped by the famous we'll buy prestige and clout as well. A recent Sunday *New York Times* devoted almost a full page of text and pictures to an article about Jan Kushing, a prominent socialite whose parties for Cabinet members and Senators were alleged to cause beautiful New Yorkers to fall over each other for her invitations. She was quoted flaunting the high desirability of her guest list and the sultry secrets of her success. Some of the highly-placed names she dropped subsequently denied even having time to answer her phone calls, and the very people she was trying to impress made fun of her. Still, most of them agreed that her publicist had done his job well. She

47

may have called the opposite kind of attention to herself than she meant to; but she did achieve a place out of obscurity. "People may hate her, but they'll go to her parties anyway because so many people have heard of her now," explains one socially sought-after mediacrat; and even her social competitors agree. Being known for being known is sometimes enough. New Yorkers forget frauds sooner than heroics. After all, the fraudulent Clifford Irving still gets invited. So does John Dean.

In New York the name-famous are hard to distinguish from people of substance. Those who in their private moments are writing or sculpting or performing heart transplants or inventing cures or making progress are indistinguishable in a fame mosaic from the utter objects.

Newsweek's cover spread of Diane von Furstenberg contained several pages of color photographs of the designer's private life: posed on her bed in a leotard, posed with her children in the park and at breakfast, posed with the also famous Marisa Berenson, Dino De Laurentis and Jean de Noyer stiffly and elegantly seated on a couch beneath a tryptich, a Warhol silkscreen of the princess designer wearing what she offhandedly refers to as one of her little bourgeoise dresses.

Was the evening contrived? Are we to believe this is an impromptu moment? Or is such curiosity out of place? Diane von Furstenberg is indifferent to such questions. Her friend Warhol taught her that the most bourgeois thing in the world is to be afraid to look bourgeois, and picking up on his double talk, she flaunts her fame in the face of middle class American women who buy the little bourgeoise dresses with the closeup of her face on the tag.

Because New York is an arena where so many trends are set, and because most of its players move too fast to pay very clear attention to details, when a genius goes public, he promotes his art or ideas by reducing them to slogans. Otherwise, one reasons, how will he get noticed? In New

48

York, Warhol, Capote, Mailer, Steinem, von Furstenberg, and others are all masters at playing the one-liner fame game—reducing big ideas to popularized concepts. Politicians forfeit depth for the sake of credibility. Even well-meaning celebrities who try to offer their fame to a cause they believe in sometimes sabotage themselves. When Leonard Bernstein invited the press to his home to push the Black Panthers, and Tom Wolfe wrote up the "radical chic" of the party, Leonard Bernstein looked not like a fame philanthropist but a self-serving fool. This image upstaged the politics of the evening, advanced Wolfe as the country's reigning satirist (more because of the term "radical chic" than the thought behind it), and nevertheless *helped* Bernstein advance the Panthers to advance their message.

For the fame observer, this is where the fun starts: a famous composer/conductor moves out of his fame slot to make famous a band of political renegades, whose cause is both cheapened and enhanced by the attentions of a "new journalist." So the moment transcends all participants and pertains only to what is famous, what is acceptable, what is trendy or news-making or controversial or flaunted.

In the same way, when Lillian Hellman appeared in the pages of *Vogue* and *Harper's Bazaar* and the *New Yorker* posed in a coat made from the skins of a herd of mink with the caption beneath it: "What Becomes a Legend Most," Lillian Hellman, a legend in her time, left behind her acclaim as a playwright, her political censure, moral triumph, back-biting gossip, flattering autobiography. The woman who had snapped in the face of the congressional committee of McCarthyites: "I cannot and will not cut my conscience to fit this year's fashion," slipped into the fame-mannequin slot in the show business tradition of Bette Davis and Lauren Bacall and Marlene Dietrich and Diana Ross, smiling for the camera, keeping her mouth shut.

Her achievements were blurred by her fur, and yet something larger was clarified. Even before her death, her legend

49

was established: Lillian Hellman, well-dressed for posterity.

So the world of principles is a fame statusphere indistinguishable from social prestige, fashion, singing, acting, moviestarring, conducting, restauranting. The fight for fame blurs the distinctions between hype and commitment, between success and stardom, between glitter and insight, between illusion and reality for posterity.

Fame in New York tempts many seekers to fake even the bare essentials from the start, but since professionals have the skills and props pretty well tied up, do-it-yourself methods often fail.

A middle-aged heiress to a Pittsburgh fortune, when she was at an elegant West Coast reducing spa, became intimately involved with a young Italian man on the staff there. She tried desperately to lure him to come back with her to New York. At a candlelit low-calorie dinner she presented him with a shoebox full of money to buy a Jaguar XKE, credit cards to buy a wardrobe, and a contract with a top publicist in New York City. The young man claims that it was during her explanation of how that publicist could get him anything he wanted that he decided to return the shoebox and the credit cards and stay where he was. But socially ambitious newcomers to town hire publicists to make them famous the way their forbears kept social secretaries to keep themselves obscure.

"The work is not the fame. The money is not the fame. . . . I don't know, I'm afraid to think about it," admits Elaine Kaufman across the backgammon table to Jules Feiffer, who shrugs:

"You start out working," he mumbles back, "and suddenly you're famous and you don't know what part of your character is making you famous. When you sit back down and try to hit it again, you don't know what to do again. So you do honest work if you can, and if you're lucky it keeps you up there."

50

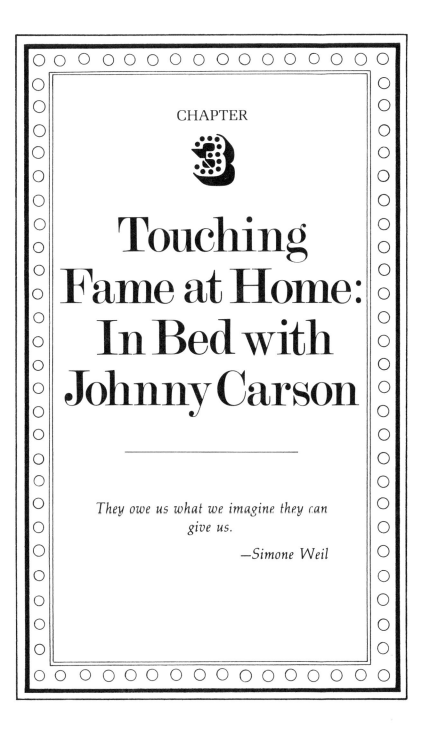

CHAPTER

3

Touching Fame at Home: In Bed with Johnny Carson

They owe us what we imagine they can give us.

—Simone Weil

Television images fly in and out of dreams, usurping fantasies, simultaneously adding to and subtracting from intimacies. When we wake up in the morning, we flip on a broadcast that tells us what will go on during the day; we come home from work and unwind with the news; and as we go to sleep at night we share our beds with the guests of Johnny Carson.

We count on television rituals just as regularly as we count on our lunch breaks and our turns in the bathroom. Some of the figures that appear regularly on television are more important to us than people we share our lives with. They usher us into an officially established reality. The more often they appear, the more famous they become and the more we depend on them. But there's a trick: we in the audience are locked apart from the performers at the same time that we are locked in the same room with them.

Although we may feel we know these fame phantoms in some human way, we know even better that they're total strangers. Still, since they have access to what's new before we do, since they get to talk directly to each other, the closer we can feel to them the closer we feel to reality central, and so we enjoy the illusion that they are part of our lives. Closeups of their faces, specific details of their lives, their manner-isms and their voice patterns are accessible to us morning, noon, and night; but their physical presence remains as remote and untouchable as the center of the universe that they seem to be hooked into.

Television appearance has become a way of officially existing. *I am electronically projected into the private homes of millions of my countrymen; therefore I exist. I show, therefore I am.*

Johnny Carson is television's fame herald. He invites people he thinks the audience should know about to visit him and he talks with them right where we can see them. "The Tonight Show Starring Johnny Carson" supplies a public rite of passage from obscurity to officialdom for the fame hero. Although he would deny it, perhaps because he denies it, Carson is America's priest of fame.

One function of a priest is to define the ground rules for his flock, in some cases to actually redefine personal experi-ences, even as Thomas Aquinas defined guilt and the apos-tles defined virtue. The peculiarities of private life look more acceptable and graceful once we see them writ large *on Johnny.* When Carson snickers at sex jokes, our discomforts become fashionable too. We feel more acceptable, freer, better. Only a chosen few of us will actually be invited to walk in and join him for a talk. That invitation, the chance to *do Carson,* to be *on Johnny,* is tantamount to a blessing.

"Johnny Carson is royalty," explains one promoter, "the king of show business. If Carson puts his hand on your shoulder and says you're acceptable, you're welcome to the court. Then, in your resumé, in your ads in the trades, it says you've *done Carson* and your agent turns into a bigger agent and goes to the producers and says *'This fella has done Carson,'* and the producers sit up and take notice."

Public appearance on Carson's talk show is worth more than money and prestige, it is a mystical transformation in which a fame seeker becomes a fame hero, a legend in his own time. Between commercials, Carson bestows the wreath of fame on questers the way Cronkite bestows official reality on random happenings, the way priests bestow the sacraments of marriage or communion or death or sainthood.

Carson's nightly ritual of conjuring up fame, repeated with precise form and ritual, salaams, fanfares, drumrolls, "*Heeeere's Johnny!*" night after night after night for more than a dozen years has been heard often enough that it casts a spell: it is hard for an audience or a performer to call a person famous until his image has blended into the fame mosaic of "Tonight," being shifted from the hot seat next to Carson to the next and the next until off camera the image joins the audience in the blurry obscurity of watching the ceremony. Carson's constant and repetitious welcomes, his glib questions and wisecracks would not be riveting from an ordinary person; but Carson manages to juggle his writers and hoofers, their wit or bad taste, and end the show singing arias and balancing a bicycle on a lower lip in a way that keeps us watching.

Carson himself is insulated from the guests before and after their on-camera talk much as the oracles at Delphi were kept from the bearers of riches in ancient Greece. And whether drugged as were the Delphics or stone-sober, his is the voice of the oracle. He provides time and space and words for an endless procession of questers who come bearing their flattering hopes and treasures; and after leaving the ordained couch, guests feel they have participated in something which was significant enough to change their lives and separate them from the rest of their countrymen.

And millions of other vicarious fame pilgrims take these figures into our homes simultaneously, sharing them with each other and our families, their regular visits giving us material for speculation, for worry, for gossip, for hope. They are like us. Once we've given them our private time and attention, we feel they owe us at least some of their time, and sometimes even the highlights of their private lives.

We get both more and less than we deserve.

55

Tiny Tim, a psychologically undefended falsetto singer, flaunted *on Johnny* a helpless vulnerability, perhaps even a glandular imbalance, a naive and demonic charm. He filled the fame slot cut by Milton Berle's Arnold Stang and Steve Allen's Don Knotts: the innocent freak.

By making Tiny famous, Carson officially freed him from shame, liberated him and through him freed the audience from some of our terror of the grotesque. Carson as he sat chatting with Tiny seemed more in control of life than ever.

The Tiny Tim wedding *on Johnny* was the first full-blown real life spectacle that Carson tackled. It was something of a risk expanding the talk show forum to include real life. When a health food promoter died from a heart attack on the Dick Cavett Show, the producers decided to forfeit the irony and shock appeal and never aired the segment; but Carson's bureaucrats decided to promote the spectacle of Tiny Tim's wedding, the slick celebration of the innocent freak in all of us; and it worked. According to the ratings, America loved it. The grotesque made us feel safe because we could tell ourselves it's only show business, he's not really like that, the unwashed hair, the girl's voice, the tiptoe. The freakish innocence cloyed and scared us enough to keep us watching, but because we were able to focus on the *artiste,* we let ourselves enjoy ourselves. When Tiny Tim, the overblown adolescent, strummed his ukelele for his beloved bride Miss Vicky, we congratulated him and we congratulated ourselves.

Tiny Tim never seemed embarrassed; and the fame and credibility he gained from the Carson appearances—temporary as they were, subject as they were to the whims of Carson's producers—were genuine, on a par with that of the politicians, musicians, and actors who appeared with him.

Craig Tennis, former talent coordinator for the Tonight Show, found Tiny Tim for Carson. He believes

You should always go for the unknown. There is a time when a performer is right for the show, and there is a time when he is no longer right. It's a kind of magic instinct to be able to tell the time for someone, and Johnny Carson has that magic instinct.

To appear on the "Tonight Show," to get a few minutes on the airline lounge couch next to Johnny himself, is a real *coup de fame.* The guests get to be performers and audience at the same time in public. Carson maintains that he has endured as long as he has because he is a reactor—he defines himself as a member of the audience. Yet the part of the audience that he represents is the most demanding part: if a guest lets a second lapse, Carson is right in there making fun or doing a double take. Maybe that's why Carson himself is so skeptical about audiences. He has said, "They root for the underdog until he gets on top. Then a lot of people start hoping he'll fall on his ass."

Herschel Bernardi is one performer who learned the hard way. He was a Broadway star, the central character in a television series. The first time he appeared on the Carson show, he became earnest, opened up and flopped. He learned quickly and painfully that an audience does not want to hear that an actor works hard, that he sweats, that he argues with his wife and children (unless one can caricature the vicissitudes of being human in the entertainment world— like Robert Blake). So Bernardi and his wife, Cynthia, invented a personality for him to project. They made a list of rules: Always wipe the sweat off before letting anyone see you. Never admit you are tired. Smile all the time. When you have no idea who someone is, say "Nice to see you again."

Subsequently the Bernardis, like Tiny Tim and Miss Vicky, were divorced. The effects of fame games on the human relationships of performers as well as their audiences can be bloodcurdling. "The mask got stuck, I guess," says Cynthia Bernardi in retrospect. "The man I married disappeared."

Whenever there is a third party—imaginary or real—let

alone a camera, a band, a highly-paid cheerleading producer behind the camera, and a culture hero to your right, it is hard to be yourself. A first-time guest remembers the experience as a dream:

> I was there suddenly and Carson was next to me and I heard, 'da, da, da, da, da,' the intro theme, and then the jester monologue, and then in a few minutes I was led— as if in my sleep—up next to Johnny. And he asked me questions I knew before he'd ask me, but it was the way I've felt hundreds of times at home when I watched it from my bed, half dazed, asleep, or near orgasm with my old lady. I couldn't talk straight; he asked me perfect questions, he was the perfect host, but I wasn't ready for him. I fumbled, I couldn't believe it was happening.

According to Craig Tennis, very few performers understand what their obligation is on a talk show.

> They can be deadly dull and assume that mentioning their adolescent daughter's acne is fascinating. Some people know how to wrap up a story in their adolescent daughter. Others don't—they'll just say "She looks so good in yellow!" and assume that's a story. It isn't. Being yourself is terrific only if you're an intrinsically amusing person, and very few of us are.

Tennis explains that it's up to the talent coordinators to help the visiting talent look good on camera by giving them drinks and reassurance before their entrance. Once when Tennis was teasing Tony Randall about his costume before the show, Randall advised him, "You're doing the wrong thing, kid. It's very hard for me to go out there. Don't try to make me laugh by insulting me. Cheer me up."

Shelley Winters, a consummate actor, projects what seems to be a tenuous grasp on self-confidence; and she does it often by a series of illusions. One night when she was to appear on *Johnny* she looked in the mirror and decided she

58

could not let the public see how much weight she had put on. She called her publicist, Arnold Lipsman, from the dressing room. "Look," Lipsman told her, "just wear a black dress and tell them you were instructed to gain weight for your role in "The Poseidon Adventure."

Winters did just that, and there followed a deluge of letters from indignant fans who chastised either Winters or her fascist bosses. She served as her own prop and it worked.

So the talk show romance between performer and audience is rooted in appearances which often are confused with facts, contrived either by the performer or his agent or Carson's pre-interviewer or talent coordinator or spur-of-the-moment by Carson himself. But members of the audience make odd assumptions even without conjuring tricks. Diane Keaton, who plays up what she claims is a very real vulnerability each time she appears on *Johnny,* is swamped after each appearance by letters from viewers offering to protect and take care of her and make her feel better.

Some guests seem to indulge themselves in public narcissism for more personal reasons, transforming the opportunity for self-exposure into a therapeutic experience for themselves. No sooner did Totie Fields have a leg amputated as a result of a serious illness than she made the rounds of the talk shows telling jokes about her trauma, apparently working out over the air some of the problems of amputation. Likewise Edye Gorme will tell how awful she feels that her husband Steve Lawrence is off across the ocean making a movie with a gorgeous young starlet, making her feel old and threatened. Or Paula Prentiss mentions that she has had her contraceptive coil removed recently so she and her husband Dick Benjamin can have another child.

As host and guests appear to be chatting casually, they are of course carefully prompted by experts; and we in our mobile homes or suburban split levels, apartment or tenement compartments, in beds with or without earphones, prone or sitting or engaged in procreation itself, receive the ritual of "The Tonight Show Starring Johnny Carson" and let them redefine reality for us.

But on the set of the in-person "Tonight Show Starring Johnny Carson," religious analogies dissolve. One feels embarrassed, like a child who for years lived with wild wondering about the thumping he'd heard in his parents' room, and when—by the time he mustered up the nerve and went in and peeked—saw that, despite his imaginings, all they were doing was sleeping.

An innocent fan somehow expects the actual in-person performance of the "Tonight Show" to reveal itself, as if the hundreds of versions we've watched in our bedrooms were just an introduction. And we imagine discovering what is really true, the substance behind each innuendo, the friendship that buttresses each joke. We want to learn what Joan Rivers, Peter Falk, and Mel Brooks are *really* like.

But behind the scenes there is no real human contact: the performers are systematically rehearsed and cloistered beforehand in their tiny separate dressing rooms. Then they're let out one by one as if from a starting gate by a talent coordinator assigned to them. And by the time they reach the hot seat, they're ready for an ordeal. But before they know it, they're directed to move over a seat to make way for the next guest, and then it's time to go home.

Carson has said that the moment one show is over, his mind races ahead to what he'll do on the next; and it's clear that all his concentration is on his performance on-camera. Carson believes that a performer stops growing when he walks off the stage, that it's dangerous to stay away from an audience for too long because "the audience keeps growing and you're just a day older than you were the last time you performed."

Surprisingly, the people who produce the "Tonight Show," although they speak about Carson either in hushed tones or with great cynicism, are very straightforward when they talk about putting the show together.

"We have nine slugs to fill up, that's all," explains Howard Pappish, another talent coordinator, referring to the spaces between commercials. If the staff creates the illusion of intimacy, of relating—at least of visiting, at most of *attending the host*—it is because the nonchalant tension sizzles at the proper moment. "Johnny can tell even if someone's been great fifty times, he'll say at fifty-one, 'I think the person's running out of gas,' and he's right. You can tell by what happens to the hair on the back of your neck—it's gut reaction. The show has a mystique. Johnny has magic, and he has a sixth sense."

Another more cynical producer explains,

If you have a talk show, you are bombarded by people whose job it is to get people and products on the air. You try to read every periodical that exists so you can understand the trend, what people want before they know themselves. Because you can get very wrapped up in your product. And the host gets very confused about who they are and what their mission is. I don't think there is one talk-show host alive who doesn't start thinking he is a very special person, that he has questions above and beyond the ordinary person, that he is entitled to things beyond the ordinary person. Some think they're going to actually change the world to the way they think it should be.

Carson fights this impulse and insists he's here to entertain. That's why he's outlived Paar and Allen and Cavett.

The staff's job is to discover or create interesting stories the guests can tell while they pre-interview each hopeful months and weeks beforehand. Tennis explains:

The pre-interview is sometimes done on the phone, sometimes they come to your home (i.e., the performers'), or you come to the studio. These guys have files on every personality. They can tell you everything you've

61

ever said on that show before. There are five pre-interviewers. They have to be smart. It is amazing how much a personality will reveal himself to a pre-interviewer. So they'll say this area embarrasses me, or I'd like to avoid this, or let's push this part. Like with Peter Falk—"don't ask me anything about my life, I'm getting a divorce."

Once the stories have been established in the pre-interview, Carson gives the leads and bounces one-liners on the show. He never greets a guest before air time. He simply assumes that the guests are there because they want people to see them, to buy their product, to recognize that they are special and worthy of being looked at, to reinforce their own hope that they're famous enough.

Carson promises to produce—right after the commercials—his guests—the immortal Sammy Davis, Jr., the legendary Mel Brooks, defining the substance of legend and immortality in terms of entertainment. The fame grail is not just the honor of being a guest *on Johnny,* but to be invited back often enough to be named a legend, even given the additional honor of being a stand-in or *guest/host.*

Guest/host is in itself a word that bulges with the duplicities of the talk show and distracts from Carson's personal pressures and need for time off. No wonder—the pressures mount to such a feverish pitch before airtime that for the sake of his health and sanity, Carson needs frequent breathers to keep himself fresh and vigorous when he's on the show. In fact, once for a gimmick, a cardiologist wired Carson to measure his heart beat. During most of the day it measured within the normal range, but right before air time it showed a significant increase. This, according to former talent coordinator Craig Tennis, indicates the pressure, the surge of tension, the seige Carson undergoes before every performance, apparently believing he's not been alive, not grown a moment since he was last out there.

62

Tennis goes on to describe the staff's sensitivity to Carson's moods.

It used to be that when Carson was in a bad mood, John Carsey, one of the directors, would always pick up on it. Once, a few seconds before air time, Johnny snarled at him and immediately Carsey pretended his watch was a wrist radio and said, "Honey, I think it's all over here, don't buy the puppy for the kids." Johnny melted and walked out onto the stage laughing, and it was all okay. But unfortunately Carsey left the show. Now Pat Mc Cormick tells Johnny a shit joke. It's not as good but it works to break his panic.

Tennis further explains the dynamic tension which works in Carson's favor. "Carson will not even shake hands with a guest if he runs into him in the wings before the show. He *wants* the terror. It's what makes him effective."

"Entertainment is like any other major industry; it's cold, big business," Carson has said. "You become successful as I see it only if you're good enough to deliver what the public enjoys." But Hollywood's fame truth—giving the public what it wants—takes a different form in television, whose strongest function is to recycle reality as entertainment. Television officializers are much more frank about their purpose than politicians who insist they seek audiences only as part of their job, never for fun, never for profit. The fame-makers of the entertainment world are not ashamed of seeking attention. "What's wrong with being hungry to be watched?" they ask, seeing no difference between news and entertainment, or between entertainment and exhibitionism.

No wonder Carson works so hard to seem non-threatening. Look at the illusion he presents: that people are simply sitting around schmoozing because they want to; that the audience is getting a peek at the *real* people; that he's enjoying himself; that the guests are enjoying themselves; that the audience is a welcome guest too; that Carson himself is a member of the audience. His contrived neutrality allows his viewers to perceive fame as liberation or as therapy or as salvation—or all three.

In some ways, he sounds like an industrial realist, but incorporated into his work is a sense of magic. To wit, his comedy character, "Karnak the Magnificent," who holds "hermetically sealed" envelopes—a fetish he shares with the bestowers of the Academy Awards—and tells the answers to questions in the envelopes without even opening them. He says, "I'm not sure where we got the name Karnak, except that there's a temple of Karnak, and it has a magical sound." So Carson, by walking the thin line between technique and magic, assures himself a multi-million dollar annual salary. "When I'm onstage, I'm on. That's my job: being funny."

The gushing of a Merv Griffin or the audacious chumminess of a Barbara Walters, like the arch shyness of a Dick Cavett, apologizes for the formidable position of the fame usher. But Carson knows he is in big business and he knows the difference between romance and work. Romance is the job of the audience. Work is the job of host and guests alike—if a guest doesn't acknowledge this ultimate fame truth, if he doesn't do his homework and prepare his image for an appearance on "Tonight," if he succumbs to the pressures or glamour of big-time fame that a guest shot on Johnny creates, he becomes an instant fame loser. He is never invited back.

The risks for the guests are even greater when they realize that no one on the show cares about them—or their fears, their nervousness, their expectations—but that everyone (guests included) is simply obsessed about Johnny. Indeed, the whole production is orchestrated to make Johnny "feel good about himself," including Severinson's warning to the studio audience that "sometimes when Johnny appears people get so excited they forget to clap. Please remember to clap. Johnny needs your applause." So even the audience is nudged into the high anxiety level that the show must go on, and in order for it to go on everyone has to help.

The ambiance of the program itself, with its blazered pages and bustling technicians, is like the boarding gate of an airport. Hard though it may be to imagine, there are thousands of Americans who believe that Carson is sending them secret messages when he blinks both eyes and looks straight into the camera. Carson himself is annoyed by viewers who write letters showing misunderstandings of his performance; but his personal annoyances are irrelevant to the show and he knows it. What is relevant is the business of being on. The fact that Carson may perform the deadpan blink as a carefully developed comedy technique, or that he is appalled by the mail he gets from strangers is his own business.

Televised intimacy has advantages for both performer and audience, allowing each to pull whatever is fancied from public talk. Part of Carson's job as he sees it is to keep his awareness of the difference between romance and work—between magic and technique—a secret.

Home viewers watch Carson's small talk tableau and wonder what his guests are like in real life; and we, mistakenly, assume that Carson himself knows or cares. One reason Carson can sustain the tension of a decade and a half of doing the same act is because he never claims to have the inside track. He is as innocent, he maintains, as the rest of us. All he knows is how to do a good job.

Johnny Carson sees his face in the studio monitor and hears the applause of a studio audience. The audience in the studio and at home look at Johnny and see our friend, the most regular fame tease in America, and hear him inevitably begin his program with the simple, deliberately mediocre stand-up monologue, the effect of simplicity deriving more from his delivery than from the content of the material.

I have no power, he silently promises us. *Sure, these famous people come to visit me and I share them with you all; but I'm not really sure of myself. I'm not really a fame priest.*

He pretends he is swinging a golf club. He shrugs. He

65

seduces us. We buy his regularity and then as a reward for our applause of recognition, he tosses us the kind of duplicitous one-liner that is both arrogant and humble and that keeps us coming back for more:

I know just how you feel, folks. I felt that way myself the first time I saw the Statue of Liberty.

The trading in of intimacy for public talk means faking effortlessness, denying the sweat, the nausea, the addiction to one's own adrenalin, the impulses of the obscure self that cries out to expose itself, to give the audience something they can squeeze. Just as the show is a religious experience for its audience, it deeply affects the performer. The talk show pact not only can obscure the difference between performer and audience, between private and public life, but it can also render virtue, intelligence, politics, depth, ethics, intimacy and art irrelevant.

Television performers claim to be startled by the sensation of the approach or assault of people who recognize them and ask not only for their autographs but also for their advice or reassurances. Carson is asked for his autograph in urinals. Total strangers drag their children over to him in restaurants so he can watch them tapdance.

Perhaps, ironically, one of the hopes that may have led the fame priest to success to begin with was the chance to tell the whole world what was on his mind; now he reads other people's versions of what he has to say. And he can only keep up the fame if he goes softly on the things that matter most. Only with careful orchestration, then, does a man like Carson provide the chance for Americans to escape from the limits of our own private lives and at the same time grant us the voyeuristic fantasy that we're sharing in graceful, important moments of people who matter.

Becoming an authentic talk show personality comes to mean for performer and audience alike accepting the illusions of public image as reality: So fame has come to mean importance. Visibility and volume stand in for innocence and virtue. Because the American dream is rooted in romantic myth, performers as well as audiences, questers as well as ordinary mortals respond to the promise of fame the way all romantics respond to greatness. We struggle. We swoon. After all, instant fame could mean instant immortality. Performers go home trying to stay faithful to a public image, grateful to their audience for acknowledging it. The audience goes to sleep with passing gratitude for the performance, imagining we see in "Tonight"'s fame mosaic our private lives writ large.

"Tonight"'s elaborate and constant slugs—safely beyond the realities of the home viewers—sustain the mutual fantasy that fame brings fulfillment. Systematically locked into the romantic myth, we can all keep our illusions about the power of fame as long as our reach exceeds our grasp.

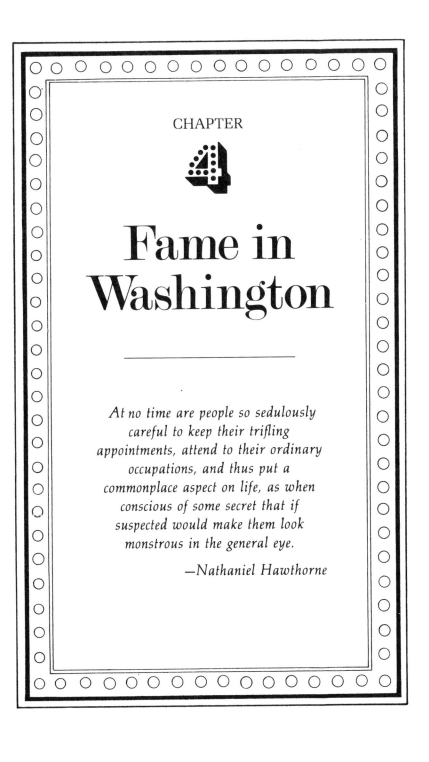

CHAPTER

4

Fame in Washington

*At no time are people so sedulously
careful to keep their trifling
appointments, attend to their ordinary
occupations, and thus put a
commonplace aspect on life, as when
conscious of some secret that if
suspected would make them look
monstrous in the general eye.*

—Nathaniel Hawthorne

1

The Lay of the Land

Washington is an artificial community, a statusphere held together by the assumption that power is a virtue. The tension is intense between the government people and the press, who traffic in power politics or the keeping and telling of secrets, and the socialites, who think power is tied in with name and social position. Political power is abstract, much more illusive than high salary or glamour or touchdowns. And the quality of experience in Washington mirrors that abstraction.

Fame in Washington means publicly appearing to have power or access to power through a highly developed series of poses. Because power is invisible and can become a target for kidnappers the minute one flaunts it, it is seldom flaunted. Therefore, the most famous—the people reputed to be closest to the center of power—are not necessarily the most visible. Their fame, like their power, is not billboarded as it is in Hollywood or spotlighted as it is in New York.

Everyone in town is playing in at least one of the three fame arenas: social, professional, or public. And in Washington, the most humorless of all American cities, the fame game is played for keeps. Lawmakers here see themselves as full-time makers of history, "and so do we of the press see

71

ourselves as the writers of history; we all are on a crusade for the good of the American people, and we take ourselves very, very seriously," says columnist Jack Anderson.

The making or writing of history brings one to the very edge of immortality. And the promise of immortality looms not only from Arlington National Cemetery, where the vast Kennedy hill dominates everything, but also from the name plaques of statues and office buildings and bills, and in the stacks of the Library of Congress. "It's a heady business to be responsible even for a single sentence in a tax bill," says congressional aide Jim Dolan. "That's the justification for a lot of the drudgery and pandering that go on here."

Fame fantasy in Washington, then, is living beyond one's lifetime, changing the course of history. And the quest for fame does not belong to government officials or the press—it touches everyone.

"I may not go down *in* history, but I've gone down *on* history," states Elizabeth Ray, who, after a failed attempt at Hollywood fame, returned to Washington to expose herself and gave us all a peek at a seedy side of power. In a way, she *has* changed the course of history, although she was accused of being interested only in financial gain and nothing more. But it was fame Ray went after—fame stripped of virtue, truth stripped of beauty—and the nature of her accomplishment is a fantasy many of us share. Whether she was more right or more wrong than Wayne Hays, she will be remembered long after he is forgotten—not because of what she was, but because *she gave us a peek.* We will forget what she looks like, but we will remember her image. And future members of Congress will behave differently than before. That difference may only be superficial, but still Elizabeth Ray—former prostitute, model and groupie—will die knowing she has made a difference.

Power through diligence is an old American virtue; and in Washington, the most overtly Puritan of all American cities, this is especially true. A senior officer at the State Department says, "In a bureaucracy you work hard, you can't leave before the boss leaves and the boss hardly ever leaves. There is a lot of need for caution in this town too, you want at best to keep your job or even more likely you want to move up. Ambition ties into work here; you do your work and you plan to do more and bigger work. Work has something to do with power, the power to get things done."

When people on Capitol Hill or in the State Department describe power rushes, they talk about the old-fashioned thrill of being called "sir" or "ma'am" by a military man or being greeted by name by the Speaker of the House. They describe making people hustle for them and manipulating people to get what they want. Kissinger called power "the ultimate aphrodisiac," and used his power to get fame and his fame to get more power. He could juggle socialites, academics, spies, and diplomats. He could openly interrupt Middle East peace powwows to lunch with Taylor and Burton. Although he is rather plain physically, he has wit and charisma, and he is a master at dancing the fame tease. "I never would ask Henry Kissinger what's new," says Jack Anderson. "He'd never tell me."

In Washington, government is the business of the show, and, as in all versions of the fame game, performers and audience keep shifting, tossing their roles back and forth among themselves like a hot potato. Sometimes the performers are government officials, lobbyists, professional constituents, bureaucrats and attorneys. Their arenas are the floors of the House and Senate, the White House, the various department offices, the restaurants and social events.

Then there is the press, which acts as representative of the public audience that the politicos claim to represent. The press reports to the public on the performance of the government officials, but the government officials are watching the press at least as closely as the press is watching them. It is obvious that the press depends for the business of its show upon the doings of the government, but it is surprising

to discover how intensely and intently the officials scruti-
nize the press—partly for entertainment, partly to find out
who's who.

Until recently, the social elite in Washington consisted
only of local rich people who are called cave dwellers
because they own and live in Washington's oldest mansions,
and who pride themselves on being listed in the Green Book,
Washington's social register. They consider themselves aris-
tocrats by virtue of their real estate and financial holdings,
and look down on the more temporary and opportunistic
types like senators and media people. It is with great pride
and high placement on the thrill scale that the cave dwellers
reject "temporaries" and "newcomers" like Elliot Richard-
son and John Chancellor when they apply for membership in
the exclusive Chevy Chase Country Club. The cave dwellers
enjoy very little power except to flaunt their permanent
claim to social position to the government types and the
press.

But media access is beginning to render the power of the
social snub meaningless. Social events are superseded by
media events, and the cave dwellers have to adjust to the rise
of the mediacracy. In the same way that the press people
convince themselves they're serving the country and are not
in it for fame or their own prurient interests, so the cave
dwellers believe they're contributing to the community as a
whole by providing the social network. And in a way they
are.

Old-fashioned status parties are still given by cave dwellers who in fact control the use of the halls. There is value to
old-fashioned society ambiance for government officials. It
preserves the illusion that social events exist for pleasure
and not for business. It disguises espionage as gentility.
Socialites perpetuate the illusion that grace and hospitality
exist for their own sakes and not as a means to an end.

But the players (cave dwellers, government members and
press) are really more complicated than they seem, as they

juggle illusion and reality for the sake of posterity. And sometimes one's own fame juggling flies completely out of one's hands. Gossip is stronger than the press and powerful press agents.

To wit, Robert Kennedy once walked into a party where he knew virtually no one. When introduced to Ronnie Eldridge, he recognized her name, kissed her and thanked her for a couple of favors he remembered she had done for his campaign. Ten minutes later he left. Because their kiss was public, her access to him became famous and she got the reputation of having Kennedy's ear. When people wanted favors from him, they telephoned her. She always insisted— and still does—that she never had that access, even though in Washington circles everyone believed that she did. For instance, at a restaurant not long ago, Eldridge was introduced to Daniel Patrick Moynihan, who was sitting at a nearby table. Meeting her, Moynihan rolled his eyes, nodded and took both her hands meaningfully. "Ah yes, Ronnie Eldridge," he sighed. "Bobby Kennedy loved you so!"

If gossip can make someone seem powerful and therefore famous in Washington circles, so can strategic exposure to the press start the ball rolling. Barbara Howar, brief darling of the Johnson administration, admits in her memoir *Laughing All The Way,* "For me, happiness was national exposure: being in front of the network television cameras at the Johnson-Humphrey Inaugural while I danced with Lyndon Baines Johnson in full view of millions of people, enjoying the Walter Mitty dream of Washington women. I was *that* woman dancing with *the* President. Those fifteen minutes in Lyndon Johnson's arms elevated me from obscurity. For, whatever else the old Commander-in-Chief may have been, he was highly skilled at wrapping a leg around a dancing partner."

Just as the appearance of proximity to power can bring fame, lack of social visibility can provide an image of power or access to power. The first night of the Cuban missile crisis,

Jack Kennedy and a few of his key men did not appear at scheduled dinner parties, but no one thought much about it. The most intense reaction was a pang of disappointment, because the social power people had a hard time finding fill-ins for last minute cancellations. When the same White House figures did not appear the second night either, it became clear that something was going on at the power source. The third night dozens of lower echelon figures canceled out too so it would appear that they too were powerful enough to be involved in the crisis.

The illusion of effortlessness is a speciality of those *born* into social fame; it is that birthright, which resembles nobility, that provides the ironic link between the almost extinct cave dweller and the emerging class of the newly famous. The image of effortlessness is usually cultivated by the newly famous, for unless they've achieved high fame and kept it awhile, their rough edges show. They can't hide how much they enjoy their fame. So they keep the old guard around as models for effortlessness.

But behind the scenes a lot of effort goes into most social gatherings. At the Kennedy Center or at embassy parties or elaborate affairs for visiting dignitaries from abroad, cub reporters who show up for a free meal can get a glimpse of a Kennedy or a cabinet member or his boss. But simply being in the same room with someone doesn't mean you have access to him or to his information. There are highly developed ways Washingtonians climb, trying to meet each other, bribing each other for introductions so they can claim the next week to have met so-and-so at a social function. Others trade favors for arranging actual sit-down lunches or dinners, or strategic ways for a lobbyist representing, say, an oil company, to sit down with a stickler from the Environmental Protection Agency.

The laid-back members of the younger set sometimes serve on paper plates and sit on the floor, but that doesn't mean social evenings among the famous and powerful are ever spontaneous. Only the style is shifting. So the grand-children of the exclusive crowd that used to find itself at Pearl Mesta's mansion on Saturday nights now meet on Sunday mornings at a corner drugstore in Georgetown by invitation only.

If one is invited, one attends. According to a frequent bruncher, "No one would dare refuse." You may see Ben Bradlee there with Sally Quinn, and uninvited drop-ins range from Lauren Bacall to Dustin Hoffman. The host is Doc Dalensky, a pharmacist, not a Pentagon chief. His drugstore is neutral territory, and has the aura of informality about it, but it serves the same function as stuffier dinners at fancy homes. And it provides a chance to perform and absorb in a pose of off-duty candor.

Nevertheless, the formal cocktail party hosted by the established cave dweller is still the most respected medium in Washington for the exchange of gossip about power, jobs, romances—and secrets.

2

An Exclusive Party

"Yes, well, and you know, so now. . . ." Elias Demetracopoulos, middle-aged Greek financier and obsessive guardian of Greek democracy, is riding in the salon of a dark brown Mercedes 600 limousine sipping a Coca-Cola. His hostess, Deena Clark, heiress to the American Volkswagen fortune and local talkshow hostess, sits across from him with her back to the driver, and takes ice cubes with silver tongs from the silver mirrored bar beside her and drops them into an engraved crystal goblet. She is teasing him about being a gadfly.

"I had to look up the word 'gadfly' in the dictionary this morning," he tells her. "I understand it means an elusive devil." He sips his Coca-Cola. Deena Clark winks and pours herself some more vodka, explaining that the Polish ambassador had it delivered that morning to Arcadia, her Washington estate.

"Yes, well, and you know, so now. . . ." Demetracopoulos looks triumphant. Just this morning the *Washington Post* has revealed that Nixon's dirty tricks committee had considered him a "dangerous gadfly"; that an anonymous memo seeking to discredit him had been sent around Congress with the help of the State Department in 1971, when Demetra-

78

copoulos had attempted to have aid cut off from the Greek dictators. Although a key staffer on Capitol Hill had shown him the memo and he had demanded and received a written apology from Assistant Secretary of State David Abshire nearly five years ago, it is only today that the incident has been made public.

"I don't even mind being called a dangerous gadfly, but I do object to the word 'lobbyist,' " Demetracopoulos says. "I am not a lobbyist, I am not paid by the Greek government. I have been offered the U.S. ambassadorship of Greece, and I have turned it down. I work for the Greek cause out of love, not money. I make my money from Wall Street."

Deena Clark shifts her bare shoulders and crosses and uncrosses her legs under her gown. A beam of light shines from her diamond earrings into Demetracopoulos' glass. "Oh, Elias, nobody knows the real story about you, all we know is you're fun!"

"Yes, well, and you know, so now. . . ." Demetracopoulos crows. He is sleekly handsome, immaculately dressed, European, rich, full of credentials. And he is a bachelor. He smiles at her and recalls the night in 1971 when they attended a charity ball, the very day he had learned about the memo.

"How did you wait five years to leak it?" she asks him, dipping her head to wait for the answer.

"I had," he says solemnly, "to sacrifice my personal honor for the greater good of Greece."

"You are a hero, Elias," says Deena Clark. "You really are You're the only non-American who will be at the Burke's party. Sometimes I wonder why we invite you. Our lists are so carefully regimented, you know, we only invite selected admirals or generals or sergeants and those things. Oh no," she scolds herself, "we don't ever invite the sergeants, do we, we just go to the movies with the sergeants." She winks and moves her shoulders back and forth.

Demetracopoulos finishes his Coca-Cola, places his glass with the seahorse motif back on the mirrored bar across from him, and rubs his hands together. He asks if it is true that Ms. Clark has over a thousand seahorse artifacts in her living room alone.

"Yes, I have, but they don't overwhelm one, do they, Elias?"

"No, not at all, your home is magnificent, as befits a woman of your stature. You know, 'Deena Clark' is a famous name, not just a cave dweller. You are famous for that, but you are also a very intelligent woman, a woman of intelligence, well, and you know, and so now we are here."

The Mercedes 600 floats to a stop. The chauffeur opens the door, and Ms. Clark lets him take her hand and help her down from the car. She and Demetracopoulos walk across the lawn to the modest red brick house of Admiral Arleigh Burke, former U.S. Chief of Naval Operations. He greets them at the door, scolding Ms. Clark as she reaches for his tie. "Stop that! I hate women who straighten my tie! I wear it crooked because I like it that way." And then he takes the hand of Demetracopoulos. "Well, Elias, congratulations, my friend, it's all coming out now, isn't it? You're a man of great patience." He turns back to Ms. Clark, but she has already gone inside to hug another admiral. So he says to the next arriving guest, "You know, this is quite a man. He saved my neck once fifteen years ago and I didn't find out about it until six months later."

Demetracopoulos claps Admiral Burke on the shoulder and shakes his hand some more. "Do you realize you have said that in front of the Chief of Naval Operations of the United States?" he asks. Burke goes on, "I'll say it in front of Vice-Admiral Holloway and in front of my dear wife and I'll say it again. This man stood by me and told the truth and I didn't find out about it until much, much later."

Demetracopoulos looks as if someone has just given him a kiss. "I am honored, Admiral, to hear you say that."

Demetracopoulos circulates, stopping to talk with retired Admiral Charles R. "Cat" Brown, whose eyes fill with tears. Brown, former Commander-in-Chief for the Sixth Fleet in the Mediterranean, has lost his ability to speak as the result of a massive stroke. He takes the Greek's hand and presses it to his cheek.

"Good to see you, Cat, you're looking well," lies Demetracopoulos. Then he says to the Admiral's wife, "You must bring your husband to have dinner with me at the Jockey Club. He is a great man; we were together on many occasions when he was leading the Allied forces."

The woman nods. "Why, that's very kind of you, Elias."

"Yes, well now, and so you see. . . ."

"Elias, there you are!" A woman in a flowered dress adorned with an enormous orchid greets him. "We read about you in the paper, you know we were very proud of you . . . You must come visit me sometime soon so we can talk." She is referring to the palatial quarters she shares with her cave-dweller husband. Her corsage is homegrown.

"Yes, well now." He bows.

"All right, Elias, you son of a gun, what do you think you've won this time?" asks Admiral Francis Blouin, of Nixon's National Security Council, former liaison to the CIA. Blouin quickly withdraws at the approach of David Abshire, Assistant Secretary of State under Nixon and author of the formal apology to Demetracopoulos which Evans and Novak called "unusual." Abshire is much taller than Demetracopoulos. They shake hands.

"So, Elias, what do you think of the Greek situation now?"

Demetracopoulos shoots back that he is severely concerned, that the anti-Americanism in Greece is growing and growing, that the American Navy is no longer welcome there, and that the Greek government is sliding to the right again just on the eve of Tito's death.

Abshire nods, either from indifference, confidence, or to cover his embarrassment.

Demetracopoulos continues. "I am not a man to bask in the glory of having told you so all along, but I must say to you that I am not surprised and so well, now, you see."

Deena Clark reappears to announce she is leaving for

another party and that she will send her chauffeur back to pick up Demetracopoulos in an hour.

"You are very kind, my dear," he says, kissing her hand. "Enjoy your evening, all the best," and he snaps back to the conversation with Abshire who, since he resigned from the State Department, has become head of the Georgetown Center for Strategic and International Studies, one of the most powerful think tanks in the country. Probably Abshire left the State Department for reasons having little or nothing to do with Demetracopoulos. But it is clear that he considers him a man to be reckoned with since he must wonder how Demetracopoulos managed to get hold of the secret memo in the first place and then get such diverse people as Senators George McGovern and John McClellan and Congressman Benjamin Rosenthal to go to bat for him. He will probably never know the answers.

Since the number of jobs in Washington is limited, secrets—especially the story of professional gaffes—are valuable. People are afraid that personal publicity can cost them their jobs, and are afraid of other people's fame insofar as it could usurp their own. But history books have room for many names, and one way of playing the fame game in Washington is to reassure people that in spite of considerable ambition you're not after their jobs. Demetracopoulos, because he perserves at least the illusion of being an outsider at the same time that he has mastered the social, public, and political fame games, can show up anywhere. No one is sure just what it is he's after, but at least it's not a job. He's got a good job.

Demetracopoulos' eccentricities put other people at ease, so they talk openly to him and tell him what he wants to know. And because he is omnipresent, he is useful to them as a source of gossip. He learned the rules of the fame game early on. His interviews with Barry Goldwater and Admiral Burke, syndicated in hundreds of American newspapers as well as in Greek ones, infuriated Jack Kennedy and Lyndon

Johnson and increased his own visibility as well as that of his subjects. So he walks in high circles, but his tiny room in the Fairfax Hotel is shabby, piled with xeroxes and newspapers. His real concern is Greek power; and from the appearance of his Greek passport and transient's living quarters, one suspects that the job that really interests him is in Athens.

In 1967, when the fascists seized Greece and muzzled the newspapers, Demetracopoulos quit his job as a journalist, escaped from Greece with the assistance of the United Nations, and gave his brains and access to information not only to the Greek crusade for democracy but also to Brimberg and Company, a Wall Street firm that now pays him a rumored $100,000 a year to be a "dangerous gadfly." He reports back to them and their clients on all the political, military, economic, fiscal, and congressional developments in Washington he can get his hands on. While it may seem odd that a non-American is paid so well to advise Wall Street bankers and investors about the affairs of their own capital, that is Demetracopoulos' gift—he is an outsider and he pays attention with the intensity of an exile.

His job opened doors no lobbyist could ever enter. Wall Street knows he is biased, and his employers treat his interest in Greece as an allergy or eccentricity. He is skillful enough at his job so that they pay him a generous salary, and he works hard and loyally for them because it gives him the money and entree he needs to work for Greece.

But there are those who doubt that Demetracopoulos is as benign as his image. Young Greek radicals who think the cause of democracy belongs to them suspect Demetracopoulos' high connections and presume he is funded by the CIA. Paradoxically, the Washington Post story shows how much of a threat he was to the CIA as well as to the Nixon administration and the State Department. Diplomats say the State Department still takes Demetracopoulos much more seriously than it does the Greek ambassador. When the

83

editor of *To Vima,* the most prestigious newspaper in Athens, visited Washington, the Greek ambassador invited all the key journalists and government officials he could find to a reception given in the editor's honor. The only "A List" invitees who showed up at the embassy were Clifton Daniels of the *New York Times* and his wife Margaret Truman.

But when Demetracopoulos threw a bash the following night at the estate of his friends, the Walter Marlowes, it turned into a major social occasion. The attending guest list included twenty-two ambassadors, thirty-four members of the House of Representatives, forty-two senators, and most of Washington's prominent socialites, financiers, newspaper columnists, editors, television journalists, and bureaucrats.

Demetracopoulos' party was the talk of the town. In Washington, inner-circle fame is a proper tool for one so disciplined that he could withhold the secret about the "dangerous-gadfly" memo for five years. Yet strangely, in fame's terminology, it is not Demetracopoulos' disciplined power-playing but his label as a dangerous gadfly that is perhaps the highest accolade one could earn in Washington. Flitting from one party to the next, escorting talk show hostesses, and sharing seemingly casual conversations with senators and admirals, Demetracopoulos presents the pose of effortlessness and gadfly savoir-faire while at the same time he accomplishes the most diffucult task the fame game offers: the trading of secrets.

3

The Art of Public Secrecy

Washington's most intense fame moments oddly enough are almost totally invisible; personal not in the California sense of self-indulgent feeling but in a more abstract sense that bridges business with smugness and gossip. What is announced or leaked is almost always a distraction, a deflection, a cover for something else. So gossip is never idle chatter. And like all name dropping, gossip is an essential mode of the audience in the fame game. Press aides are hired to let drop rumors or leaks and announcements that distract from incompetence or dullness and keep a name in the air. As Jack Anderson says, "The ability to mold public opinion is what gives you power in a democracy, so the Presidency is stronger under fame people like Kennedy or Roosevelt than under a Ford or a Nixon."

But the ability to mold public opinion is moving now from the politicos to the press, who after Watergate seemed to acquire a more direct line, more of a right of access to the ear of the public than ever before. The press is no longer considered a simple vehicle of what the politicians say—indeed, after Watergate it couldn't afford to be. Meanwhile, the politicos feel an increasing loss of public trust: as the polls contrive to show that large percentages of American voters believe that politicians do not tell the truth. So the press tells its own version. And when Woodward and Bernstein exposed Nixon, in a sense they usurped not only his power but the power of the Presidency itself. They leaked the Great Secret.

The relationship between power—invisible and abstract—and secrets—also invisible and abstract—is complicated. A rule of the power-fame game is that something must always be held back. Maybe it's nothing more than a mistress or a lover, but secrets are the coin of the realm, the dexedrine that spurs Washingtonians on to work. Secret-keeping can at least bring prestige and at best bring power. The next best thing to knowing secrets is to seem to know secrets.

Secret-mongering is full of contradictions, buttressed by the sense of power of being the one to tell someone something he didn't previously know. The good self-promoters are the ones who seem only to be leaking a little bit, to be holding back what they really know for another time. They are the ones who get invited back again and again for more secrets, or whose columns get read again and again for more items, or whose bylines get more and more prestige because they find scoops. The leaking of a secret can be as theatrical as a curtain call. So it was with Demetracopoulos, secret-keeper and secret-giver all at once. He knows the rules.

Woodward and Bernstein—before they out-famed the famous in Washington, when they still had noncelebrity status—acted on the assumption that the most titillating news is gathered under cover. It may well be that Woodward and Bernstein took home the cynicism and technique of press agentry and invented Deep Throat, the famous nonentity in Washington, to protect and preserve the real gossip sources within the cluttered echelons of Washington.

And just as fame-mongerers in Hollywood and New York hire publicists to advance their image, so do Washington politicians use underlings to leak secrets and advance their power. "There are many people who enjoy the exercise of power but would lose that power if they got credit and not their bosses," explains Jack Anderson. "People who really run the bureaucracies have learned to keep their heads down below the visibility line and allow their superior to take full credit for everything."

"The political figures are usually satisfied not to exercise the day-to-day power—they can have the fame, and would just as soon not be bothered with the details. But it's understood that if the underlings step forward and take credit for their own secret manipulations or recommendations of policy, they'll lose their positions; so they smile obsequiously, subordinating their national craving for credit and publicity, and get their official credit by putting the clause in the tax bill, and their power thrills by leaking secrets."

What Woodward and Bernstein did in making famous the secrets of Nixon fulfilled and fed the fantasies of what most of us want to do with people more powerful than we are. Peek. Peeking is the impulse, the job of the audience, and it is at the core of the fame game in Washington. Whereas most of us feel somewhat guilty about wanting to place our ears to bedroom doors, Bernstein and Woodward came out of the dirty laundry room smelling like roses. When they speculated about the sex or drinking habits or peculiar undignified moments of this first family, they justified even the pettiest, most prurient wonderings by tying them in with great crimes against the nation.

Woodward and Bernstein are the champions of the Washington fame game. They invented their own fame slot: mediacrat stardom. What Redford and Hoffman acted out in Hollywood was their story exactly as they wrote it: no PR middlemen, no outside mediacratic reporters to distort their story. Woodward and Bernstein, without visibly moving a muscle, got their own versions of their own stories acted out for them. Then they sat in the audience opening night and watched America's favorite movie stars *pretending to be them on their own terms.* They achieved the *coup de fame*—being performer and audience simultaneously.

When Woodward and Bernstein turned voyeurism into a fame virtue, they gave greater legitimacy to all levels of the mediacracy—from social gossips like Betty Beale and Sally Quinn to political gossips like Jack Anderson.

Beale is unabashedly serious about her work. She believes firmly in snobbery and name dropping as healthy methods of survival. And although she might not call herself primitive, her defenses and aggressiveness epitomize the old-fashioned socializer. Popularity is as important to her as to any cheerleader, and she thrills to the magic of two powerful people in the same room with her and nearly swoons when they forbid her to quote them.

By contrast, Sally Quinn is no swooner. She has mastered the fame game. People are frightened of her sharp tongue but nonetheless grant her interviews because a mere mention of them under her byline is enough to indicate that they are important. A whole front-page article by Quinn in the "Style" section of the *Washington Post* is a ticket to social posterity. A perhaps more transient fame moment, although certainly a more intense one, occurs when Quinn attends your party without portfolio. An evening with Quinn off the record is Big Time for people secure enough to exchange public fame for small group fame.

Elected officials cultivate gossip to keep their names alive. They have several constituencies to perform for: the staff, the back-homers, the social scene in Washington, the interest groups. And they collect from them when it's fund-raising time and butter them up by hanging out with them. This is a full-time job, and it keeps them constantly straining. So the power of the gossip columnist in Washington reflects the fact that public officials are vulnerable to obscurity. When they collect from their audience it's not just for an Academy Award or a good score, it's for the right to stay in business. The fame business is an addicting one. Thomas

Eagleton explained, when asked about the nervous breakdown he suffered after he was elected Attorney General of
Missouri, "You have to understand, there were no more
crowds, there were no more cameras; I was stuck in Missouri
and I had nothing to do."

As with the talk show, or the Academy Awards, the
pursuit of gossip appears to be a celebration of status. It is
instead pure, self-serving business. In the Fame Age, one-to-
one performances are rare, and the knack of being direct has
been lost. Because the quality of life in Washington is
abstract, because eyes are always glazed over with terror
and caution and eyestrain, piggy-back celebrity is worth
money and votes. Gossip is the social power of the new-
comer and Washington is a community of newcomers who
leave and return with the regularity of elections.

No one is a better newcomer-watcher than Elias Demetracopoulos:

> I knew John Mitchell would be a failure in Washington
> when he had his secretary phone the president of the
> Seelgrave Club—the oldest and most distinguished
> women's club in town—to get Martha accepted there. He
> might have been a very successful bond lawyer in New
> York, but he didn't understand the rules of the game in
> Washington.

But gossip in its most formalized manner of exchange
sometimes creates an expectation of trade-offs which, when
expressed openly, destroys the value of the secret gossiped
about. Jack Anderson, eating a tunafish salad, phone in hand
(the White House has him on hold), a reporter's tape re-
corder on the table, a television crew setting up across the
room, explains, "We have people who insist on being mentioned in exchange for a story; we fight against it. There are
sources who don't want to be named for obvious reasons,
and there are people who want to be named but not as
sources. They want some visibility, some credit, some atten-

89

tion in the column. Their payoff is that they want a story written about them that we might not ordinarily write. We've had congressmen and people in power give us stories and say 'I want my name to be mentioned in a specific paragraph.' "

What Anderson doesn't say is that these congressmen have hired freelance investigators who make a career out of finding dirt—in government agencies, lobbying groups, blue-ribbon commissions—and selling it to power-hungry politicians. And what about these and other stories that don't get told? We're told in whispers and in news releases that the whole truth about the assassinations of Kennedy, King, and Kennedy have yet to surface, that the real Watergate scandals still remain secret. Maybe that's the reason political villains can hold their heads up and write their own exposés. Because what we don't know can't hurt them. There's always some secret saved up in Washington; the illusion/reality game is always under somebody's control.

The big rule is never to seem surprised when responding to the telling of a secret, although it is often proper to feign surprise. Acting is an accepted form in Washington: spontaneity is frowned upon. Doris Kearns, in her biography of Johnson, recalls him

> explaining how he varied his act with different reporters, that Stewart Alsop cares a lot about appearing to be an intellectual and a historian—he strives to match his brother's attainments, so whenever you talk with him, play down the gold cufflinks which you play up with *Time* magazine, and to him you emphasize your relationship with F.D.R. and your roots in Texas, so much so that even when it doesn't fit the conversation you make sure you bring in maxims from your father and stories from the Old West. You learn that Evans and Novak love to traffic in backroom politics and political intrigue, so that when you're with them you make sure to bring in lots of details and colorful descriptions of

personality. You learn that Mary McGrory likes domi-
nant personalities and Doris Fleeson cares only about
issues, so that when you're with McGrory you come on
strong and with Fleeson you make yourself sound like
some impractical red-hot liberal.

An air of detachment pervades this town of professional
representatives. The pose of emotional indifference smooths
out moral wrinkles and makes people glad to have you on
their side. "Grace under pressure," they call it. So there are
few people in Washington who are openly passionate about
the cause they are working on. "It's not considered professional; you figure the coalition of forces on either side is
going to change. And that if one is a professional about it,
one realizes that today's adversaries may come in handy
tomorrow," explains one lobbyist who, unlike Elias Demetracopoulos, is proud of his mercenary salesmanship.

To people in Washington it was not remarkable that
William Ruckelshaus was an aggressive champion of environmental concerns. His reputation was built on the fact
that he took the Department of the Interior—which really
had no power base of its own, and which a lot of people in
Washington wish had never been created in the first place—
and was successful in pursuing its interests as head of the
Environmental Protection Agency. But no one asked if these
interests were good in themselves. Ruckelshaus was respected because he built a power base for this particular
interest.

"But what happened when Ruckelshaus left EPA and
joined a law firm representing industrial companies?" our
lobbyist continues: "The fact that he went, if you will, to the
other side, to the oil interests, doesn't detract from his image
in the eyes of people here. Rather it's the normal progression
of things. He was also successful later when he represented
Weyerhauser's interests, and that, too, was considered
proper. Having been successful on one side of an issue he

91

became a person that people on the other side pursued because he was an effective advocate."

Just as issues are morally abstracted, Washington people seem to think of themselves and each other as titles and jobs and names; so friendships are based on opportunities, and sexual liaisons become business transactions. It is hard to imagine either the chance or the impulse for Washington professionals to fall in love, and if they did, to indulge in such passions as love may inspire. Clearheadedness is a virtue to Wasingtonians in the way a sleek suntan is in Los Angeles or prodigy alertness is in New York.

In each version of the fame game, performers risk falling flat on their faces; and maybe that's why so many people who are drawn to fame prefer the safer backstage positions. In Washington the risk is in public elections; but in spite of all the media flirtations the real work goes on backstage. Even the people who are at center stage are famous only, they insist, as a sideline. Nevertheless, "What the senators are doing up here on the Hill is perpetuating an image, and they don't dare do anything contrary to that image," explains Robert McCormick, who covered the Senate for NBC for thirty years. "It's no wonder these guys have secret drinking rooms and hanky-panky rooms—they need to let off steam."

"Everybody's watching," explains one Capitol Hill image off the record. "All of the time, either to see who you're talking to and try to figure out who's lobbying whom and who's trading favors, or who's flirting and who's slipping up. It's not just competition or the press, it's the tourists walking in and out of your office representing the public you think you're serving; and you constantly have to be receptive and distant at the same time. You never know who's going to decide to write a book."

The strain irritates, but it is also enormously ego-inflating. Some members of Congress spend a disturbing amount of time rewriting their remarks for the Congressional Record, putting things in the Record that were never said, polishing their prose. Hang around Capitol Hill long enough and you believe you're at the center of the universe.

Speaker of the House Tip O'Neill was greeted recently at an airport by a man with the words, "I suppose you don't remember me . . ."

"Hey, fella," O'Neill reportedly interrupted, "that's unfair. I'm constantly meeting people, I'm on television a lot, I'm over six feet tall and have a big red nose, and people remember me. Just remind me who you are and don't apologize, okay?"

The younger man apologized. "Well, we had dinner together last Wednesday night. I'm Robert Redford."

And O'Neill apologized: of course, how could he forget. But when the man left, he turned to his aide, and asked, "Who's Robert Redford again?"

Because their lives are so stuffed with busy work, social appointments and obligations, all elected officials have staffs who serve as prompters. The aide of one prominent member of Congress compares Capitol Hill to the court of Louis XIV. "There were thousands of courtiers and their life there was choreographed from the time they got up in the morning to the time they went to bed at night. And there were certain events that they were expected to participate in, in order to remain a member in good standing of the court. Expected modes of behavior at that time extended to the way one dressed, what one said, what one ate, whether one knew the new minuet.

"The courtiers were expected to be on hand when the king awoke in the morning. A person was particularly blessed if he was able to hold the royal garments while the king put them on. These positions were very carefully doled out and they didn't happen by accident. Someone would hold the king's shoes or hold his cloak. Well, here in Washington there is a similar pecking order. Certain people must be jumped for not just in terms of their business activity, but

93

also for their whims, their desires, their actual care and feeding."

Different players react differently to the pecking order. One leading member of Congress avoids parties where bigger shots than he appear, and makes the rounds of the smaller-time social circuit, always accompanied by an escort. His escort, who also serves as his administrative assistant and social secretary, explains, "Once I find out who else is invited to a given event, research goes into what my boss can say to each interesting person, so that there will be the basis for a conversation, so that he won't be caught in a corner, trying to think of something to say. All this is worked out beforehand. For example, when Dimitri Rostropovich was finally able to emigrate from the Soviet Union, he was adopted by official social Washington as a drawing card for events, and so people naturally wanted to meet him. Not because they were particularly interested in meeting him, but because they knew that the other people who would be there would be significant.

"It was my responsibility to find out something about Rostropovich so when my boss met him he could say something that involved his history, where he was from, the type of works that he had composed, complete with titles. I even did some research into what the critics said about his composing and technique. I wrote down on a card some of the phrases that were used. I recall that one of them was that he was a musical technician. Well, my boss used this in talking to him, and it evidently caused him great pleasure. I suppose that from an objective point of view that this was posturing. But to other people in Washington who were attending that event, it was not remarkable that my boss was posturing. What was remarkable was that he had taken the time, that he was careful about this sort of thing. This is what people remembered, not that he knew enough to spout off about Rostropovich, but that he had taken the time to find out. So people went away from there saying, 'That member of Congress is careful.' 'I wish I'd done that.' So I got a whole weekend off as a bonus and there was no negative judgment against him, though perhaps in another setting it would have been looked on as showmanship."

Washington is a man's town. Political secret-mongering is male gossip. Most of the women who have jumped into the Washington arena settle for sexist treatment just as the men in Washington settle for absurdly demeaning treatment based on their image. That's why the fame game is so intricate here: the way you seem is the way you agree to seem to get what you want. You dress the way you are expected to, you marry the way, you entertain the way, and work the way, and talk the way, and walk the way, and one day maybe you'll have an effect on a tax bill or a civil rights bill, you'll make that difference, you'll make it all worthwhile. You write off the drudgery and pandering and holding back because one day maybe you'll have a chance to let it all out when you've made it to the top. It's no wonder that Gerald Ford's final campaign gesture was to sing the University of Michigan football fight song: football, war, legal battle, social nicety, all codified, all masquerade. There are elements of the plot of the fame game in Washington; and the substance, what makes it worth it, is the hope of Making A Difference. Not tonight, or for any one given moment necessarily, but for history, for the rest of America, forever.

The ultimate secret in Washington is not sexual lust, not power lust, or even fame lust, but lust for immortality. It is that lust that makes senators rewrite their words for the *Congressional Record,* hold back their anger and contempt for the competition, work to exhaustion, attend pointless parties, flirt with columnists, tease the journalists, spend hours listening to tedious, nitpicking legalistic debates.

Fame does not bring the freedom to indulge in feelings or to dive into new ideas. The payoff is the possibility of going down in history, touching immortality, leaving a name on an office building or a national monument or a law. Fame in

Washington is the promise of living beyond a lifetime, outliving the voters and socialites, the courtiers and the competition. And the ultimate fame fantasy—immortality—dilutes the tedious ritual of everyday life.

When a Washington fame figure looks across the Potomac at Arlington National Cemetery, he feels the challenge of eternity. The Presidency is the only guarantee of permanent fame, and the chances of capturing that one are slim. Besides, as everybody knows, Jack Kennedy stole the show. He invented the blur between power and fame and made immortality a media event. History will remember his reign as Camelot, smoothing away the rough moral and emotional textures, turning history into a sex and violence movie in which the audience perceives neither pain nor pleasure, only spectacle. The only fate worse than death in the nation's power capital is eternal obscurity.

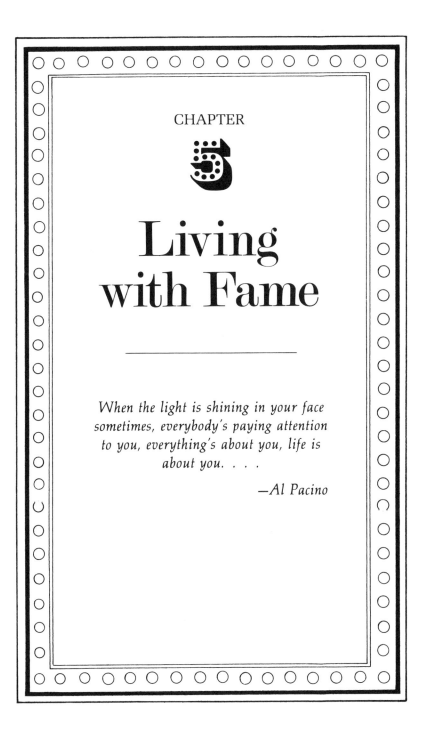

CHAPTER

5

Living
with Fame

*When the light is shining in your face
sometimes, everybody's paying attention
to you, everything's about you, life is
about you. . . .*

—Al Pacino

Paul Newman and Joanne Woodward live with their children in Westport, Connecticut, when they are not in Hollywood or on location. They are both gifted actors, both famous. Newman is more famous than Woodward. Strangers rip his glasses off his face in restaurants, tear at the cuff of his pants when he comes down the stairs of an airplane, beg him for autographs, insult him when he refuses.

Woodward says she hates being married to a sex symbol, that in spite of her own accomplishments she goes regularly to a psychiatrist to stay convinced that she deserves to live with the man millions of other women think they want.

Newman and Woodward claim they feel most at home in Westport. Among those neighbors who are aware of their fame and its side effects, they try to cut through it and be just folks, even though strangers buzz in and out of their driveway hoping for a glimpse of their privacy, and the socially ambitious invite them to be status ornaments at local dinner parties. Sometimes their children scream at cars that slow down in front of their home: "Paul Newman doesn't live here! Paul Newman doesn't live here!"

"Hi!" Newman greets a local couple whom Woodward

99

had met first and invited over for drinks, "I'm Paul New-man." And when Newman offers his hand, in spite of himself, the man responds as if Newman were name-drop-ping: "No shit!"

But there is something touching about the plight of a famous person trying to pass.

"Come for a swim!" Newman invites a neighbor lady the next morning when she comes to call for her children, playmates of his children.

"Oh, I couldn't possibly," she responds, "I've gained ten pounds since I bought my bathing suit, and I'd be embar-rassed to go out in public that way."

"No problem," he tells her. "Joanne took the kids for ice-cream cones, there's nobody here but me."

"Can he be for real?" wonders the woman, frozen into stage fright and memories of the fantasies she's had about her neighbor over the years.

What does "for real" mean to people who spend much of their time being public images? What is the everyday feeling of fame? Is it possible to slough off fame's unspoken threats and demands which define social expectations for audience and performer alike?

The self-conscious neighbor is caught like a snapshot in the double bind of awe and suspicion. Like her, we in the audience have consumed so many details about the private lives of total strangers that we are stuck with an official image of what they are *really like*. We think that because they have captured so much of our attention they have a power over us, a power we lack. We envy them, and that envy prevents us from understanding who they are.

Publicity photographs that show them smiling give us the sense that fame makes them happy. Yet other candid photo-graphs that show them looking unhappy—like the front page closeup of Rita Hayworth being spirited away to a sani-torium—teach us that fame makes them drunks or suicides. When we see them in person, we either shrink away or assault them. How, we wonder, can anyone who looks like Paul Newman—who *is* Paul Newman—have a normal social life in the fame age?

"The real Mel Brooks," announces the real Mel Brooks, "is six-foot-five and not Jewish; he is blond and handsome." Brooks makes a gurgling sound and announces, "that's what the stomach of the real Mel Brooks is really like." Then, switching to a more candid tone he says, "Look, of course I keep parts of myself private—even from my family—doesn't everyone?"

And privately his wife, the more quietly famous Anne Bancroft, says, "Some people think of me as the ideal woman—nicely married, famous, and glamorous. But like most women, I needed to have a baby to feel fulfilled. I'm a successful actress, I'm lucky. But still—like any other couple—when my husband comes home at night, what do we talk about? *His* problems!"

It is partially the impulse to believe that what we see is authentic that makes us in the audience so curious about fame figures. And just as some people keep secrets better than others, some of us can live more gracefully than others without prying, settling for items in *People* and Barbara Walters' reports, without wanting to know more. Thus it happens more often than not that the real pleasures of fame exist most intensely in the minds of its observers, rather than in the private lives of the performers.

Even Joanne Woodward still finds it hard to separate the image of Paul Newman from the person she married. "It's really been very difficult because it shades our relationship," she has said. "In a way you have to look at someone with two pairs of glasses. One is the reality; the other is the super-reality. Finally over the years the two begin to merge and it's very hard to make the distinction, either on my part or on his part. I mean, if you're treated like a superstar all your life, sometimes you begin to behave like a superstar, which is not easy to cope with. It is especially difficult when we are working in the same area. Anyone who says it isn't is crazy, absolutely crazy. And any woman who thinks she could cope with it easily would have to be a woman so submissive, so involved in her husband's life that it wouldn't matter whether or not she had a life of her own."

The straight talk of Bancroft and Woodward is unusual for film actresses who ordinarily succumb to the *noblesse oblige* of fame and glamour, and feel that complaint is beneath their dignity. The illusions of effortlessness and total joy are still part of the illusions of stardom for most of them, not to mention trumped-up scandal.

"If you are to succeed, people must talk about you," said Sarah Bernhardt. Like Elizabeth Taylor, Bernhardt was beautiful and talented, and she knew how to balance and enchant her public with the tease of suffering and shocking carryings-on. "Fame is the greatest whitewash there is," Taylor once said when she and Burton had tongues wagging over their behavior in their million-dollar yacht. And although we in the audience love the romantic notion that fame goddesses live in a mystical world of gorgeous and lavish success, such notions are never an accident. What Taylor and Bernhardt seem to have accepted instinctively, Woodward and Bancroft resist.

But even for people who set out to resist it, fame can be addicting. Dustin Hoffman, in Cannes for the celebration of his films, reportedly felt overwhelmed by a constant barrage of attention and ingratiation, and escaped to a remote and primitive barber shop for a shave and a haircut. After half an hour of anonymity, he felt anxious and uncomfortable and made a bee-line for the nearest newsstand, where—once he saw his picture on a front page—he could relax.

"Fame is an indication you are being heard, that what you are saying or doing matters," says New York editor Theodore Solataroff. "But you realize early on that there is another thing called 'celebrity' which is merely a lure and therefore a snare. If you're really interested in a sort of

102

THREE RESPONSES TO FAME: Muhammed Ali leans back in his telephone-equipped limousine and grins; Katharine Hepburn huddles in *her* limo and hides; Jane Fonda holds a press conference in an attempt to use her entertainment fame to influence political reality.

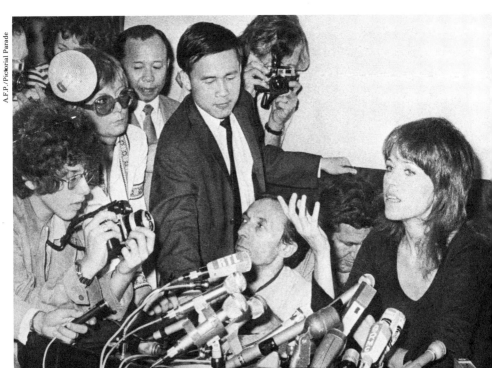

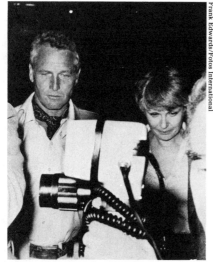

FAME AMBIVALENCE: Paul
Newman and Joanne Woodward
walk into a barrage of mediacrats
as if into combat; Jacqueline
Onassis, whose low profile is
always highly visible, appears
not to notice photographers as
she arrives at a media event with
her daughter Caroline; Woody
Allen and Diane Keaton close
their eyes as if to make the
photographers go away, while
Hollywood's Sue Mengers—not a
star but an agent—smiles for the
cameras.

MULTIPLE FAME: Henry Kissinger, master of the fame tease,
who juggled heads of state, news commentators, politicians, and
military leaders while he jetted to lunch with Taylor and
Burton, is photographed in 1972 with secret service agents;
several years later the same photograph appeared in a magazine
with a new fame role—here it is adorned with a shopping bag
from Bloomingdale's to publicize a new store opening in a
Washington suburb.

FAME MODES OF AMERICAN HEROES: John Wayne became an American hero first by portraying the movie cowboy, then by becoming a spokesman for conservative politics, cancer prevention, and Datril non-aspirin pain reliever. John Glenn made history as the first American to orbit in space, later appeared as a contestant on "Name That Tune," and still later was elected as a U.S. Senator from Ohio.

FAME'S WINNERS AS PUBLIC
SERVANTS: Marilyn Monroe
stands on her head in the sand
and smiles for America; Jack
Nicholson kneels and follows the
traditions at Grauman's Chinese
Theater in Hollywood so he can
be "permanently immortalized"
in cement.

FAME POSES: Barbara Walters, Frank Gifford (left), George Forman (center), Howard Cosell (right) attempt a pose of happy informality as they try their hand at warm-up exercises practiced by members of the Joseph P. Kennedy, Jr. Foundation's Special Olympics for Retarded Children. Barbra Streisand, Muhammed Ali, President Gerald Ford, and "a glittering crowd of national and international celebrities" also attended, transforming the event into a celebration of fame itself. (left) Dapper, charming, sophisticated, debonair Johnny Carson, the man who some say makes a living out of posing for the cameras, is caught in a rare, behind-the-scenes moment showing the strains of his job.

THE SYMBIOTIC RELATIONSHIP BETWEEN FAME AND POWER: fame as royalty—New Hollywood's queen Streisand greets England's Queen Elizabeth as fame's courtiers James Stewart and James Caan attend. (below) Fame as democracy pushed to the absurd—the Carter brothers: both are famous but only one can launch a nuclear war.

NEW YORK'S WHEEL OF FAME: restaurateur Elaine Kaufman stands in front of the clustering place where fame feeds upon fame; publicist Bobby Zarem launches and orchestrates some of America's most elaborate "instant media events." (below) Prince Egon von Furstenberg and his estranged wife Diane first became famous in New York through the social prestige of his family name, wealth, and power. Then they used their popularity to draw attention to themselves by appearing together at every media event in town. Now they use that fame to promote their "famous-name" garments. Although separated in private life, they still appear in public together— "for old time's sake," says the Prince.

FAME'S FEEDBACK: television
celebrity Telly Savalas has face-
fame as wise-guy cop Kojak, and
the public responds to him as if
he were the character he
portrays; John Kennedy's fame,
carefully nurtured before, during,
and after his presidency,
combined with the national
shock of his assassination to
make him a myth.

INVISIBLE FAME: Elias
Demetracopoulos poses with
Henry Kissinger at a
cave dweller's party in
Washington; a dressed-down
Dustin Hoffman poses with the
more glamorous Robert Evans at
a New Hollywood party. Who's
running the show is usually
invisible in the status photograph
that is snapped as a matter of
course at fame's social
clusterings.

London Daily Express/Pictorial Parade

MEDIACRAT FAME: the old—a formal press conference in the
early sixties; the standard—this publicity shot of Barbara
Walters shows authority, the "believability factor," and a
practiced smile; the new—Geraldo Rivera, a fame age television
mediacrat, prefers to report more personal, "soft" news, and like
that of many of his co-workers, his act and image command at
least as much attention as the subjects he interviews.

Raimondo Borea/Pictorial Parade

Lawrence Ratzkin/Courtesy Bantam Books

IMMORTAL FAME: Peter Finch performs in the movie "Network" as a television mediacrat whose fame-by-madness makes his ratings soar; after his death, Finch's widow Eletha accepts his posthumous Oscar and poses with Finch's co-star in "Network," Faye Dunaway, in front of a huge Oscar at the Academy Awards ceremony. Mrs. Finch's impassioned acceptance showed her grief for the loss of her husband; but his image is now immortal due to the presentation of the Oscar itself.

Courtesy Barris Productions

FAME LUST: we all have it—a senior citizen dresses up as Uncle Sam and performs for a panel of professional entertainers on "The Gong Show"; a teenager poses as media queen Patty Hearst.

Nick Allen/Pictorial Parade

FAME BLURS THE DIFFERENCE BETWEEN AUDIENCE AND PERFORMER: Woodward and Bernstein pose with their movie-idol portrayers Redford and Hoffman in a fame mosaic. Who is the star and who is the fan? (below) Andy Warhol poses innocently at his window in front of a huge portrait of himself made out of masking tape on the street beneath his studio. Warhol, a genius of passive-aggressive self-promotion, claimed that the names of the portraitists did not ring a bell.

AUDIENCE PARTICIPATION IN THE FAME GAME IS NO PASSIVE MATTER: hundreds of contestants compete to be chosen as the best Groucho Marx. (above) Marilyn Monroe's worshippers, having no access to the ceremony of her burial, watch the funeral through the cemetery fence—they grieve for the image, not for the person who just died, but their grief is real grief nevertheless. (right) Outside the Academy Awards the bleachers fill with fans who hope to catch a glimpse of their favorite stars.

FAME MOMENTS: Elizabeth Taylor arrives at the Academy Awards on the arm of director George Cukor, followed by her official escort and the designer of her gown, Halston. "I *am* the awards," she tells the crowds. They throw her flowers in response; inside the Dorothy Chandler Pavilion she sits alone, surrounded by gossip and competition, waiting her turn to appear in the yearly fame ritual.

immediate recognition, so that when you walk down the street people say, hey, there goes Ted Solataroff, then instead of staying home and working, you begin bucking to be on a television program and to be seen in the places where celebrities gather. Someone once defined a celebrity as someone who's very busy being a celebrity. It's a full-time job in its own way."

According to psychiatrist Abraham Weinberg, the constant attention, the letters, the phone calls, and the crowds are like constant noise. "You get used to it, and you think it's not important to you. And then it stops and you wonder what's wrong."

Both extremes can be upsetting. Robert Redford—Hoffman's co-star in "All the President's Men"—complained in an interview, "I hate being stared at, by anybody. Walking down the street, I feel like I'm in a head-on collision, that my life is getting narrower and narrower, and I wonder why I'm so uptight. Some of the reason, I think, is that I've lost the capacity to wander around anonymously—just hanging out, being loose, watching people and listening to them."

This fame ambivalence is as much a part of the life of a superstar as it is of the groupie. Even the Redfords and Newmans, who have made the decision to try to touch the public's political consciousness through their fame, must worry about losing its awe—after all, if you make the media mad at you, you might end up sacrificing public acclaim as well as the power to influence public opinion.

But the popularity of public geniuses like Norman Mailer, Truman Capote, and Gore Vidal thrives when the public gets mad at them. They seem to profit more and more both personally and professionally from public performance rather than from their private musings. Their fame careers are parallel but independent from their actual work, so they compete for the same space and air time with other fame players. But unlike the others, because they *want* to outrage the media and the public, Capote and Mailer and Vidal are

119

big fame winners whose outlandish performances result in giving their more serious works a continuous shot at best-seller lists.

But making fame promote work is not quite so easy for even the most famous of the one-track crusaders—like Margaret Mead, Gloria Steinem, Ralph Nader—who seem to cut through the difficulties, blending work with politics. Despite their qualifications, they are often castigated within their own fields for having no depth, for being vain popularizers. Those who would benefit from having the word spread about safety balloons in automobiles do not like the idea of seeing Ralph Nader on the cover of *People* magazine.

This, then, is the discrepancy between public personality and private self that haunts fame seekers and preys on their insecurity. Indeed, the fame arena in New York promotes that insecurity, Washington exploits it, and Hollywood pretends to make it disappear. What is the basis of it? Psychologist John Kappas believes that most people who become very famous are actually easily embarrassed—they don't want people to know what they're "really like" because they're not very proud of their private identities. Woody Allen probably spoke for many famous people when he said once that all his life he grew up wanting to be somebody else. No wonder that when the fame-seeker *becomes* somebody else in the minds of his followers, he tries to exorcise his private shame by controlling reactions through public acclaim. And probably that's why deep down, famous people cannot maintain an equilibrium and are constantly suspicious of why people grovel to them. They suspect that they're not loved for themselves, and of course they're right—because usually they're pushing something in order to hide something else, just as the exhibitionist exposes his genitals to hide something about himself he finds even more obscene and shameful. The killer Truman Capote wrote about in *In Cold Blood,* when he was about to be publicly executed for murder, was compulsively worried

120

that he'd soil himself afterwards, and what would people think?

So fame itself can serve as a private fig leaf. As long as we have the company of observers, we're safe. Attention becomes a substitute for self-knowledge, and "getting in touch with ourselves" means absorbing a public image. But then something else happens: the public image brings with it new and painful demands that tear away the fig leaf and make the famous person more vulnerable than before.

After Sandra Scott lost one hundred pounds, she was the subject of an illustrated article in a national magazine, and now when she walks around in her home town of Cleveland, strangers approach her for advice. "It is not standing out in the same way I stood out when I was fat," she says. "Now it is as though they expect something from me, simply because they've heard of me. I would have thought I'd have liked it, but it's unpleasant. I feel that I'm failing them in some way, because I have nothing to give."

What she did give them, of course, was a sense of accessibility to a famous person, but that, to many fans, is not enough. When Richard Chamberlain starred in the television series "Dr. Kildare," he was often approached in a restaurant or on the street by people who asked him to diagnose their stomach pains or backaches. Even when he explained that he knew nothing of medicine, that Dr. Kildare was only a role he played as an actor, they would nod understandingly and continue to ask him about their aches and pains. Similarly, it is not uncommon for strangers to ask the superfamous—a Cronkite or a Sevareid—whether they should take this or that job or send their children to this or that college. For the professionally famous, adapting to this confusion of image and reality is part of their job, and they handle it gracefully. But for Sandra Scott, who suddenly realized how instant fame makes people *appear* to be knowledgeable about all things, this kind of recognition only made her feel like a phony.

121

Of course, fan letters to the stars have always included requests for advice about life and love, but the truly famous hire professional letter-writers to whom they can ship the fan mail and be done with it. They get a fame bonus when their fans gratefully receive "personal" letters from them with their personal autograph (forged by the staff) on it: the fans think they are now *close* to that famous person, but the famous person is simply more isolated from the public than ever before. Thus clever celebrities can seem vulnerable and candid all at once, eliciting our loyalty without ever exposing themselves.

What is it that performers become when they are not performing? When an audience influences the way famous people see themselves and each other, their lives become imitations of an action, and the action is no longer their own. Even the family is distorted for the sake of "the public." Famous people pose with their families for publicity campaigns in artificial tableaux. The effect on the relationship of the other members of the family varies. Bergens, Minnellis, Fondas, Carradines—even Evel Knievel's son—follow in the footsteps of parents; others flee.

"You grow up knowing everybody's talking about you," says one self-mocking thoroughbred, "and you share the paranoias of the famous relative, but you aren't the one who's famous. You're invisible. So you have the hostility, you have to share the person with his public, have the dinners interrupted. But you're never equal. You never thought you were worth much attention, and then suddenly you're being looked at and admired and probed and photographed and written about and people think you're IT. But *you* know you're not.

Whether the basis of fame is that someone is the daughter of a movie idol, or has been elected to public office, chosen as a beauty queen, batted the most home runs one season, played the part of a king or a sex bomb or a derelict very well in front of a camera, private life changes to fit the needs of public image.

122

"You are a symbol," says Al Pacino. "Somebody was telling me about somebody, recently, who said, 'Al Pacino. I would go to bed with him and I'd live with him, I'd do this and this and this.' I said, 'No, not Al Pacino. No. The symbol. What Al Pacino represents.' It alienates you. You start pulling away and you start becoming what they call you, a superstar. A star. Away. Away from everything else, untouchable, unreachable."

Feedback comes at restaurants where it's impossible to sit casually and chat because fans come and press the hand holding the fork with the tomato on it, and insist on telling the famous person how much he or she means to them.

It's an impulse we all have, the urge to make a personal connection when we see someone we're sure we've known well and can't remember quite from where—it's not consciously aggressive. It comes from that same unconscious place we occupy while we're watching Johnny Carson or "Rhoda" or "Maude." These are people who have been in our homes week after week, and our familiarity seems as natural as inviting the neighbors over for coffee.

Such reactions to fame are the result of a belief in image-mankind by audience and performer alike. But this belief is not totally positive: it is as full of contempt as it is of awe. So the glee with which people claim to be sure that Capote has peaked, that Warhol has lost his genius for the superficial, that Taylor has lines in her face—is part of the attitude of the competitive fame-lecher in all of us.

The performer who believes in the image gives himself to it and lives with a regard toward his real self that is as intense as that of his clusterers. Famous people live inside the nimbus of their images, and if they seem hard for us to reach on a human level, it is because they have bought that part of the myth that tells them they're gods.

Even if people don't set out to make an image of themselves that detracts from who they really are, that image can become so demanding of them that they succumb to the insistence of the interviewer or the public, and begin to

123

imitate the one-dimensional version of themselves that the image represents. It is then that they begin to believe that superstars are the world.

Patty Hearst tells people she enjoys "sitting there in church with God watching me." In fact, although thousands of dollars are spent keeping her isolated, being watched may be the only thing Patty Hearst can count on: the *New York Times Magazine* reported on her menstrual cycle and the color of her nail polish, invading her privacy with a zeal second only to that with which they approach the privacy of Jacqueline Bouvier Kennedy Onassis.

Yet Onassis is a master of the low profile. She poses for photographers weekly—at openings, premieres, fashion shows, charities, launchings, and backstage with the stars— insisting all the while that her deepest wish is to keep a low profile. The *New York Times Magazine* obliges her, showing how valuable her image is by running a major story about her wish to be left alone, fully illustrated, with no new information.

Barbara Howar, in one paragraph of her book *Laughing All The Way* zeroes in on the prurient, often cruel, "curiosity seekers" and concludes, "certainly Jackie Kennedy was entitled to mourn in privacy." But even Howar can't resist offering her version of the cracks in the former First Lady's composure, and providing bodily details as proof of her intimacy:

Before Mrs. Kennedy was forced to leave Washington by these curiosity seekers, I sat with her one long May afternoon on the front steps of a mutual friend's house, drinking a gin and tonic, our skirts pulled up to sun our legs while our children attended a birthday party inside. There were many things I wanted to say to her, but I could not. We sat chattering inanely about children, laughing over her recollections of the days when she and Ed Howar had been in the same group at Miss

124

Shippen's Dancing Class—days, she said, when she was shy and gangling, and jealous of the "class siren" who wore see-through blouses and had "things to see" that Jackie had not yet acquired. Our only intimate exchange was a lengthy discussion of leg hair, whether it grew back faster if removed with a straight razor or an electric one. It was not a moving conversation, but probably it was the only chat with the hounded wife of John F. Kennedy that has heretofore gone unreported in the press.

Until now, of course, thanks to self-implied noncuriosity-seeker Howar. In this passage, she epitomizes the fame-seeker who hopes that fame by association will pave the way to fame by legitimate achievement. For Howar, who used her Washington notoriety as the author of *Laughing All The Way* to gain a foothold in the national televised fame arena, it worked.

Beverly Hills psychologist Irene Kassorla, who says she has become a millionairess by giving therapy to the stars, explains, "Famous people have a problem with hope. It's like the poor girl who thinks if only I'd have a pretty dress like the girl down the street, I'd be happy. And you get the dress and you say, 'Aha! I know what it is, if only the boy next door loved me,' and then suddenly the boy loves you, and it's still not enough. And the 'if onlies' increase, so if you're a Marilyn Monroe, it's 'if only they knew me in Los Angeles,' and then they know you in Los Angeles, and you're still depressed and lonely, which is part of the human condition. We need if onlies. . . . Then there are no more if onlies. Marilyn Monroe had the big house, she had the international fame, she had all the lovers she needed, she had the gorgeous cars, and she was still depressed and lonely. No wonder Monroe killed herself. Without hope, there was nothing left."

Avery Schreiber has always regarded himself as a serious comedian and actor. But for now his strongest face-fame

125

comes from commercials selling Doritos corn chips. Once when he and his family were at the beach, a group of children ran up to them and told him how much they loved him. "My children were very upset by that—and I guess I was too," reports Schreiber. " 'How can they love you, Daddy?' my son asked. 'They don't even know you!' "

So Avery Schreiber and his wife and children, who think of themselves as the opposite of elitist, find themselves taking secret tunnels under airports when they travel and selecting tables in restaurants where Avery can sit with his back to the other diners. "It's self defense," he explains. "Whenever a car follows me too closely, I worry."

What is significant is not that people are attracted to the face-famous like Avery Schreiber but that, because of that attraction, they think they love him. So it is that public information about Patty Hearst's menstrual cycle or about the contents of Bob Dylan's garbage cans or the hair on Jackie Onassis' legs can create only a false sense of intimacy. "I always forget that a person's attitude toward me is always conditioned by a lot more than what takes place between us," says Dick Cavett, who the *New York Times* calls television's most promising personality in search of a format. "Sometimes it doesn't even occur to me that I've been recognized, and sometimes people act as if I haven't. A plumber comes to fix my sink and I think, 'he doesn't recognize me, he doesn't know who I am.' And then at the end of it, he'll say, 'Well, my wife isn't going to believe this when I tell her where I was this afternoon.' And you realize, everything you said and everything he said was filtered through some other thing for him. . . . It's like there's someone calling attention to you behind your back all the time. . . . And it's like you're behind your own back waving, and making faces, so they're seeing much more than just what's there." Still, like the writer of the fan letter or the strangers approaching Richard Chamberlain about their stomach pains, those of us in the audience, when we meet or read about or think or fantasize about the famous, believe we know something of the real person behind the famous image. And, thinking this, we change our image of him and that makes him change his own attitude about himself.

George C. Scott has said in that regard, "There's no question you get pumped up by the recognition. And then a kind of self-loathing sets in, when you realize that you are enjoying it. But what is ultimately so harmful is that you are being recognized, not for the things that you worked so hard for, but for other reasons—that you're a movie star, for instance. After a while the pleasure stops, but the self-contempt stays."

"They come to me depressed and I have to hypnotize them to get them to drop the mask," says John Kappas, Los Angeles therapist, who claims to have treated thousands of celebrities. "Fame is a disease," he believes. "Its nature is the inability to stabilize." He treats primarily actors and performers who he believes got into their work and got to be good at it because they were spurred in part by an intense resistance to personal experience: they overdeveloped their masks. "When they become very, very successful, they develop a form of paranoia because then they feel that everybody likes them only for what they have and only for their image. They totally suppress the real person behind them because they themselves do not like themselves. They only like the image they project."

To psychiatrist Abraham Weinberg of New York, fame is almost always a cover-up. "Many famous people really have no identity, and they have to create an image which gives them the identity and their identity depends on their acceptance to the audience. It's just like a psychosomatic illness. Once a person develops a physical effect and lets it prevent him from recognizing his own emotional disturbance, he can focus only on this physical effect."

Theories of the unpleasant, suicide-inducing effects of fame have grown chic and oversimplified with the seeming preponderance of fame suicides: Hemingway, Monroe, Joplin, Prinze. But it is no more a fixed pattern that the famous take their own lives than that the great and powerful are murdered. What is true is that fame, by demanding so much energy, can seem to redefine reality and distract the famous from real troubles until it's too late: while the public clamors to know what they're *really like* in private, they know that there are no secrets to share, no hidden realities. Once they embrace their image and feed it out piecemeal through fake responses to fan letters and contrived interviews with the media, they return to their privacy and find nothing but image left.

Meanwhile, what happens to the audience is a continuous lust for more—more image, more peeks, more glimpses behind the mask, which, if we ever did get a glimpse behind it, would only reveal more mask. Yet this, apparently, is what we want, the *real* Mel Brooks, Dr. Kildare, Joanne Woodward, Woody Allen, all carefully orchestrated and strategically presented, sometimes funny, sometimes sad, but never naked, open, exposed. So the "journalists"—procurers of what is none of our business—descend: the Howars and the Rona Barretts, even the New Age reporters such as *Rolling Stone*'s Hunter Thompson, who during the 1968 Democratic convention waxed poetic about his once-in-a-lifetime chance to watch George McGovern use a urinal.

And then there are the hecklers.

When Saul Bellow visited San Francisco State College in 1968, his first words were, "Please, no pictures!" After his lecture, when he was asked about the self-truths in *Herzog* and then to repeat something he'd said earlier and refused, a young man in the audience—named Floyd Sallas—a former boxer, shorter than Bellow, younger, a published novelist too, shouted at him, "Why you goddamn father figure, you arrogant son of a bitch, you're all washed up I bet! You probably couldn't even come!" And Bellow, shocked and shattered, canceled the rest of his speaking tour in California, and came home to mourn the sad withering of youth and to recreate the moment in his next novel so it wasn't a total loss. The tale was retold in *Mr. Sammler's Planet* and rewritten: the heckler was transformed into a drug-peddling political activist and upstart cum villain. And Bellow, publicly undaunted, went on to write other books, transcribing his troubles into literature.

Bellow voices contempt for his hecklers and fans alike—and maintains a jealous guard on the personal life that he translates into novels. He insists that what he is really like is his own business. What he writes may draw on personal experience—like the San Francisco State incident—but that, he says, is also his business.

He won the Nobel Prize, at least in part, by paying close attention to his own fame ambivalence.

"It was my turn to be famous and to make money, to get heavy mail, to be recognized by influential people, to be dined at Sardi's and propositioned in padded booths by women who sprayed themselves with musk, to buy Sea Island cotton underpants and leather luggage, to live through the intolerable excitement of vindication. (I was right all along!) I experienced the high voltage of publicity. It was like picking up a dangerous wire fatal to ordinary folk. It was like the rattlesnakes handled by hillbillies in a state of religious exhaltation."

Bellow's idea that it was "my turn to be famous" reflects a fame fantasy that all of us have—that one day we, too, will know how it feels to be famous, to live with the adoration of the crowds, to separate ourselves from the obscurity of the *little people*. So television, always on the lookout for new ways to exploit the dreams of all the little people who view it, has invented game shows, parodies of this small-time fantasy of public appearance. Game shows provide ways of letting the audience pose as invitees, ways of pretending that the television fame game is not elite (which, of course, it is) and not limited to those who are mystically, magically, selected for immortality. But in fact, fame *is* mystery and magic, and to replace talk shows with game shows, or fame prizes (legend, immortality, blessedness) with money and vacuum cleaners works to cheapen the position of the audience. Winning a prize on "The Gong Show" has no more to do with fame than sending a message on a CB radio. What is lacking is the tension between possibility and reality, between performer and audience, between instant prizes and immortal fame.

Yet the game show winner does achieve an electronic instant of artificial fame. On television, captured for a split second in the same box that holds Johnny Carson and Walter Cronkite and Merv Griffin, the game show winner is enchanted by his own image, reflected to him on dozens of monitors in the studio and—if he can rush home in time to see the tape aired later—on the TV set right in his own living room. More thrilling than falling in love with the image of a famous stranger is the shock of seeing ourselves writ large— but not ourselves, our faces writ large—easy as pie, complicated and flat as a computer portrait, slick and superficial as Sonny and Cher. How easy it is to react at that moment as if we *were* celebrities—flinching but self-satisfied, amused but careful not to look too amused, always living inside the tension between letting go and making sure, between loving the fame and rising above it.

"Let's make a deal!" Monty Hall used to sing to the audience as he walked among them with his huge roll of bills and his elusive promises of material goods hidden behind the curtains on the stage. In the small-time fame arena, Monty Hall was as much of a fame priest to his audience as Johnny Carson is in the big time. Hall's audience would dress up in outlandish costumes to attract his attention, would swoon and cheer and weep as he veered closer to them, then away, then closer once again, to touch them and bring them forward, out of the crowd and before the camera.

Hall presented his oracles in the form of riddles and jokes, and the audience, hoping that a *deus ex machina* would swoop down from the bright lights and point to the curtain with the real prize behind it, wrought itself up in a frenzy of grotesque worship.

Today participants on "The Gong Show" dress up in similarly ridiculous costumes and present themselves with all their "talent" to a panel of celebrity judges, never asking for whom the gong bongs, knowing that in time it will bong for them, reducing them to obscurity once again. Because for them, as soon as the moment is over, as soon as the last commercial has introduced the last of the credits, the game show winners and losers can go back to their real lives and become "real" once again. No so the celebrities, who are mobbed as they walk out, mobbed the next day, mobbed by crowds as well as thoughts and fears of becoming a has-been or a flash-in-the-pan or a fame loser.

Yet for all the fears and work and constant energy needed to keep fame, those who are famous find it nearly impossible to talk about it. It is, in fact, a taboo subject, the mere mention of which threatens the equilibrium—like asking a person in love to talk about orgasm or a person in mourning to talk about death. And since fame is impossible to touch, to locate, to prove, it is no wonder that most famous people only discuss the subject with psychotherapists.

The truest believers in the magic of fame are the observers and the seekers—the audience. We're the ones who are the most romantic and the most curious about the actual, immediate experience of what it's like to be well-known for being well known. And because it's hard for us to keep track of which fast-fed information is human and which is smoke-screen or hype, we keep believing, keep wondering, keep wanting more. We think of the invisible gloom of Freddy Prinze in his Sting Ray, the short temper and charity of Frank Sinatra with his electrifying gate guarding his home, Jacqueline Bouvier Kennedy Onassis with her frozen smile

131

of stoic arrogance, and we want more. Unable to walk away from the questions of what being famous is really like, addicted to *People* and "Today" and "Tonight" and "Tomorrow," we play the fame game too, dreaming of fame and the famous, collecting bits and pieces of gossip and information, amused and titillated and sustained by television's version of ultimate fame: the Academy Awards.

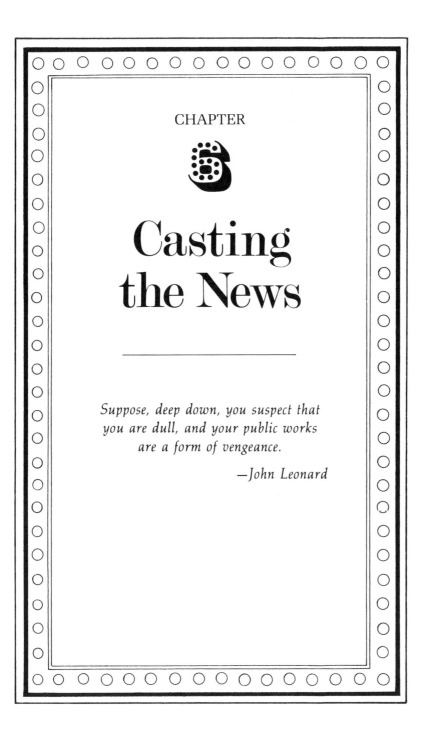

CHAPTER

5

Casting
the News

*Suppose, deep down, you suspect that
you are dull, and your public works
are a form of vengeance.*

—John Leonard

Every television newscaster who has ever reported official news has been thrust into the fame consciousness of the nation. Over the years, Barbara Walters, Walter Cronkite, Dan Rather, Rona Barrett, Jack Anderson, Geraldo Rivera, John Chancellor, David Brinkley, Howard Cosell, and others have become name famous and face famous. In addition, they have a particular kind of fame, the kind that is the most ambiguous in illusion and implication and contradiction, and in a way the most popular. Once on television, newscasters are simultaneously insiders and outsiders, straddling the line between performer and audience, worldliness and innocence, knowledge and curiosity, hubris and humility, hiding and seeking.

The people television makes famous occupy the very matrix of the fame instant, that electronic version of the status photograph. Everyone equidistant from the camera and audience appears to be equal for the visible moment, commanding the same degree of attention and wielding the same amount of fame power. Gary Gilmore brought the newscasters and their audiences to visit him in prison, pulling them away from elections and kidnaps and famous love affairs, and made the whole world watch while he got himself killed. Since the newscasters in attendance all had the same story to report at the same moment of visibility, they seemed to share in equal portions of that fame instant. But equality of fame on television is an illusion. After the execution, Lawrence Schiller—privy to Gilmore's last moments—promoted his bird's eye view and his rights to his relative's story, driving his television competitors into a frenzy of frustration. In order for Gilmore to hold more fame power, he had to die. But the mediacrat risks nothing.

Reality, *the way it is,* changes from day to day, as Walter Cronkite—high priest of newsdom—tells us at the end of his nightly announcements of official reality. News, we call his message. Newscaster, we call him, giving his job a name that sounds at once religious and theatrical.

The power of every famous person is much more limited than it looks; nevertheless, clever television interviewers know how to milk the power of fame for all it's worth: Dan Rather won his promotions to "Sixty Minutes" and "Who's Who"—the gossip columns of news programs—in the tradition of arch interviewer Barbara Walters, by catapulting himself into the rich ambiguity of mediacracy during one of Nixon's final presidential press conferences. When Rather asked a particularly aggressive question, Nixon—astonished—asked back, "Are you running for office, Mr. Rather?" The reply was that of a man with no doubts about his own relationship to his subject: "No, Mr. President, are you?" The quip created a new image for Rather, which he succeeded in carrying into other fame areas at CBS.

Barbara Walters is similarly a superb promoter of her own fame. She takes us into the homes of big fame winners in Beverly Hills and Washington and then turns to the audience and says, "Perhaps you would like to see where *I* live. This is my dining room table; this is my bedroom; this is a piece of coal from a dark dungeon of a mine in Wales. Sometimes I look at it and I think about death." By raising the relevance of her dark moments to a level of fascination

136

for the audience, Walters appears to be as worthy an object of attention as presidents and Academy Award winners.

During the last month of the Ford administration, Walters sat in the White House and said to the First Lady, "I understand you sometimes sit in the very chair in which I'm now sitting, and you look out the window and see Washington, and you feel lonely." By placing herself in the First Lady's throne, she symbolically became her replacement— only for an instant, of course, but piled up over the many years Barbara Walters has been in television are a hundred such instants, all of them creating the appearance of power. Often described as "the most powerful woman in television," she is, rather (among television newscasters), simply the most famous.

Walters told President Carter she was relieved he doesn't wear jeans to receptions for visiting dignitaries. And she brashly suggested to Barbra Streisand and Jon Peters that they ought to marry. Her awkward pushiness serves to shock and delight viewers who like to think we would never have such audacity and would fear the repercussions of such presumption. But the interviewees never bat an eye, answering her with seemingly spontaneous straight talk and the pose of fame innocence.

If Walters seizes attention away from her subjects, the subjects know how to enhance their own fame by playing by her rules. It all happens under the guise of an exchange of information that was originally created for our benefit, not theirs, but that has been turned into a fame vehicle nevertheless. So mass media broadcasts the fallacy that whatever a person flaunts is important to the rest of the world. It may be power, crime, sexual peculiarity, philanthropy, scientific headway, or it may be simply charisma: but what it is does not matter so much as how it captures our attention. On television, the difference between an attempt to cure cancer, or write the great American novel, or assassinate a President, or report it, or knock them dead on "The Gong Show,"

137

is simply irrelevant. The main point is that the American quest to achieve is now based on measurable visibility. And television news, by making no difference between image and substance, provides monumental visibility to any and all flaunters who are lucky enough, or well connected enough, or thick-skinned enough to have access to each fame instant television provides.

The audience does not object to this; indeed, because television creates its own kind of credibility, we seem to accept everything it shows us, suspending our belief that there are other dimensions to reality than appear on the evening news. But it is impossible to sustain such numbed consciousness over a very long time, so ratings based on tests of the sweat on our palms indicate that we want new fame figures constantly. Different surrogate lovers on each "Tonight Show." Different disasters on each six o'clock news. Different interviewees for Barbara Walters. And of course different commercials to intensify our impatience with the day-to-day realities of time and space: be smell-less, they challenge, be anxiety-less, drink this, rub this on you, wash your toilet with this, and you'll be slick and sexy and important, too; you'll be rich enough, famous enough, to be young forever.

It is always there, this hint of immortality, in every fame arena there is always a whisper or an allusion or a promise that fame is possible for each one of us, and that eternal youth or good looks or great achievements or mass approval will make us live longer than ordinary, dull mortals are allowed. On television news, this allusion to immortality often takes the form of religious ritual. The deaths of Kennedy and Monroe—two of America's classic tragic fig-ures—strengthened an element of martyrdom, not to a cause or religious quest exactly but rather to the consequences of fame itself. The televised Kennedy funeral, the detailed publicity of the Monroe suicide—followed by the mock heroics of the war in Vietnam, the Watergate morality play, the Franciscan humility of the Carter tableau—were all ritualized on television, broadcast over and over again in countless news spots, documentaries, and retrospective analyses as if there were a single religious belief behind them. There wasn't, of course, and in the end what survived was the sense of ritual—again, image without substance, the very food of fame.

Yet aspects of religious belief always surround fame and the famous, especially on television. Those in the audience who feel oppressed by their obscurity may think of fame as a sign of salvation, because it indicates that there are some people who are chosen or blessed by the approval of millions. So fame looks like liberation to those people who do not have money or power, let alone access or visibility—those who feel stuck in their oblivion unless they can get someone out there to notice them. Too poor to hire personal publicists, they may kidnap a celebrity's child, or assassinate a head of state, thereby feeding destructively on their victim's fate. Or they may constructively risk their lives in dangerous situations to become a hero, or work their way up in a particular field for the sole purpose of public recognition.

But there are other alternatives. If they find someone to represent them whom they don't have to pay—someone like ABC newscaster Geraldo Rivera—someone who seems to resemble them and care about them, who has public access and visibility and is willing to promote them for the sake of making the world better, they feel the promise of salvation. In most cases, these people need real power in the form of police protection, better housing conditions, health care. Instant fame may be the closest to power they can come, unless they sensationalize their protests.

Rivera argues that television fame can be used to institute social change. His hour-long closeup of pregnant drug addicts helped make him famous; and it also gave the pregnant drug addicts a new sense of themselves. They were suddenly visible—at least for an hour. Rivera claims he performed a service for the addicts and for the public as well. He made the children at Willowbrook famous too. It's not simply that he is telling the world about important human issues. He is also giving oppressed, pathetic people—official losers in a winner's world—their moment of fame.

News fame is different in quality from the higher powered, deliberate fame that people seek as careers. But clever small-timers can manipulate sycophantic newscasters, turning their human interest into good stories, and just maybe make a difference, have an impact. The desire for impact appeals to news reporters who are trained to walk into plane crash refuse, kidnap sites, collapsed mines, and criminal courts, and milk the victims.

So Lawrence Schiller is a champion fame game player. By photographing and exploiting the tragedy and vulnerability of Marilyn Monroe, Vietnam massacre victims, and the execution of Gary Gilmore, he managed to insinuate himself into the center of action, then photograph it, and finally promote not only his photos but his personal feelings about the moments as well into a profitable business. After getting an exclusive on the Gilmore execution, he and partner Barry Farrell went on television and talked about how the crass, bloodthirsty public had no idea how painful this whole job was for them: having to watch the blood dripping down Gilmore's frock after his death, talking with him earlier about murder, sensing his problems with sex, with love, with hate. But the outcome of their performance is that Schiller and Farrell have managed to have it both ways, as medi-acrats and as insiders. They are experts at how *marketable* disaster can be.

Similarly, Geraldo Rivera—who formerly called himself Gerry Rivers and then changed his name back to honor the Puerto Rican half of his heritage when it became fashion-able—when he interviews entertainers refers to their show business statusphere as "you in show business." After superstar Freddy Prinze killed himself and reality intruded into the world of fame, Rivera exploited the sensationalism surrounding the incident, writing articles and doing the round of talk shows about how he was an insider in Prinze's life, and how show business is someone else's job. Since the audience then identified with Rivera instead of Prinze, his performance had the veneer of a moral message; but the overriding effect was to put the impact of world catastrophe on the suicide and add to his own fame with the death of Prinze. This, then, is the newscaster's *coup de fame:* to insert himself into the news he reports. Rivera is not quite as good at it as Walters or Rather, however, because he lacks a certain amount of fame power. On the morning of Gary Gilmore's execution, according to a *Newsweek* account, Rivera—after being beaten out by Schiller for the last shots— phoned his bosses at ABC's "AM America" and said, as his "voice cracked urgently through the icy dawn: 'Look, it's a go, do you hear me? . . . Drop Rona, drop Rona . . . There's no time to argue. It's going down and I'll be able to hear the shots . . .' frantically trying to clear air time for the climactic moment in the Gary Gilmore story."

Since allusion to death—as the pollsters tell us—is good entertainment, it keeps us watching the news. Like sports coverage, news exploits the tension, the wish to see danger dance before us. Instant replays taunt our pity and fear, giving us a sense that we can touch the danger the athletes touch without risking what they risk: their physical selves. Part of the fascination with spectator sports is admiration for the highly developed skills of the player. But the fame element, the fame fascination fixes on the disaster wish in all of us. Bullfighting and boxing may have qualities in common with the ballet, but they have more substantial elements of pure danger. And in a similar way, tennis, basketball, even baseball—by combining competition with closeup looks at the faces of the players as they're risking everything—appeal to the fame lust, the vicarious quester in each of us. By the

141

time an athlete is past his prime and ready to write a book, he writes to the fame-hungry fan, giving us a peek at the vulnerability that was there all along. The sports books which have been most popular *(The Boys of Summer, Instant Replay)* are those that show that the athletes were not as tough as they seemed.

Bill Bradley, Joe Louis, Joe Namath, Babe Didrikson—all our famous sports figures—once their highest moments of triumph are over, survive in part by promoting an image of what is past. Their post facto survival is a particularly American phenomenon. "Didn't you used to be Joe DiMaggio?" is a question only a full-time sports fan could ask in good faith.

When television viewers see that the famous DiMaggio now drinks from Mr. Coffee, or banks at the Bowery surrounded by singing and dancing children, we easily substitute the media joys of banking and mouth washing and car driving for the more human elements of life that performers deal with off-camera. So fame survivors like DiMaggio, once they achieve perpetual celebrity status, can slip from category to category—baseball star to restaurateur to bank or coffee-maker promoter. They may be bored stiff but find adoration stimulating; or they may want to put something over on the public to get rid of an old grudge or revenge; or they may want to share a gift or talent with the world; or they may do it out of social obligation or purely for money. But whatever their motives, the real stories of their lives are always different from their public images. And even though we may suspect that Joe Namath *never* uses Brut after-shave, many of us buy it anyway because of the famous name behind it.

Television reality perpetually renews the fame blur between the achievements of athlete DiMaggio, of actor Burt Reynolds, of bus driver Ed Ray, of assassinette Squeaky Fromm, of famous daughter Amy Carter, of murderer Gary Gilmore, and of mediacrat Geraldo Rivera. They become well-known for being known; the quality they have in common is televised fame. They may vary in degrees of power or dignity or virtue or ethics. But they are all famous, and their differences are reduced to degrees of fame as their images reappear before us.

For other less-than-famous hopefuls, the false sense of importance they feel from being televised or "covered" alienates them by creating a new dimension in their lives—publicity—and then rendering that image replaceable. People on television are first defined as image, then rendered irrelevant by the sheer replaceability of that image. Expectations are artificially created, egos are inflated, and the real romance of the quest for fame—the hope, the naivete, the religious luster—is electrocuted.

Some people instinctively resist this effect of television fame. Golfer Mike McCullough tells reporters he's just not a very interesting person. Ed Ray, the Chowchilla bus driver, demanded the cancellation of the public Ed Ray Day which was to celebrate his heroism (but after the acclaim died down, he appeared on "Hollywood Squares").

Generally, ordinary people who become television heroes through tragic circumstances sense that their claim to fame-by-disaster is a chance in a lifetime for public triumph, and so play it to the hilt. And as victims of the disaster are milked by newscasters, the exhilaration of TV coverage supersedes the effect of the disaster itself and even lessens some of the pain of loss by adding an element of spectacle. Form, intensity, electronic importance eases the lonely pain of tragedy. So in the end, fame eats up triumph and disaster alike.

But if people have interesting relatives, or disasters befall them, like athletes and entertainers they command a fleeting attention. It is a mistake, then, for a champion or a victim or a singer or a mediacrat to believe that news attention can do any more than make them feel important for a while. All too soon the medium releases them to fall back into the obscure

143

posterity of small-time catastrophe arenas and overshadows them once again with Reasoner-Walters and "Kojak" and "Marcus Welby" and Sonny and Cher.

It is in their multi-million dollar weekly television extravaganza that Sonny and Cher exploit the unremarkable in themselves and in the audience. Their personal publicists promote their failed marriages, their image of glamour mixed with uncertainty, appealing to home viewers by disguising the differences between the performers and their audience. When they have finished their act, they thank the audience for being the most beautiful they've ever had. They tell us they love us. Sometimes tears come to their eyes. They look at each other and shrug as if to say, "Why us?"

Yet the luxury and voluptuousness of Sonny and Cher's sets and costumes, the elaborate floor shows, the gilt images, the big money, the pomp and circumstance surrounding their children, contrasts with the "just-folks" humility of their personas. This mock humility helps unworldly viewers identify with the gilt and relax with their easy money, to settle into the belief that people just like us can make it big, can get fame and fortune.

On television, Sonny and Cher, the Bionic Man, Charlie's Angels, Donny and Marie, the Captain and Tenille, Laverne and Shirley, Alice, Kotter, and others seem no less real in their electronic fame slots than the heroes and villains and victims of reality on the evening news. Especially now that newscasters are trying as hard to relax and entertain as much as actors in weekly series are trying to give us a dose of *real life,* it's easy for anyone to stare at the tube with numbed consciousness and mix everybody up. Or to view scenes of brutal death and disaster in Vietnam as casually as shootouts on Starsky and Hutch. Or to think that when Peter Falk makes a guest appearance on Merv Griffin he is really Columbo in person. Everyone and everything competes on television for every instant, turning newscasters into entertainers who compete with actors and talk-show hosts and

144

commercials: even with the highest of ratings, nobody wins in this arena except, as the movie "Network" pointed out, television itself, which in the end can be seen, simply, as another vehicle for fame.

Two thousand years ago, the Roman poet Ovid wrote about his "quest for everlasting fame, that I might be celebrated throughout the whole earth." How happy he would have been, had he known about television. Television, more than *People* or *Us* or gossip, is responsible for the fame age. All of us are exposed in the privacy of our separate rooms to the celebrations of celebrities. We don't need to go to Mecca, or to the fame arenas of Washington or Los Angeles or New York City, when we can turn on our sets and be transported. We can be attendants at Woodstock, Altamont, Watergate, Entebbe.

Ovid's quest for fame would have been much less of a gamble had he lived in the fame age. Millions of us would recognize his face by now, not just his name. We would know the names of what he wrote, we would feel able to peek beneath his facade while we filed our nails, polished our shoes, ironed our clothes, made love. We would listen to him chat with Barbara Walters. We would know whom he was living with, what shade of papyrus he wrote on, whether he got writer's cramp, whether he reached for his instant breakfast before he wrote a Canto, what shampoo he washed his hair with, whether he rode the bus or rented a limo, whether he had seen the King Tut exhibit and went right out and bought himself a complete set of King Tut towels and sheets, whether in his opinion Egyptian was *in* this year. Like the current public genius Gore Vidal, Ovid would unapologetically consult a publicist like Jay Allen for advice on "getting his act together" before he went on television to sell his idea and make himself famous.

Television and *People* and *Us* have rendered most of us experts on the trivial truths about many of fame's heroes and heroines. We know that Paul Newman drinks beer and races

145

cars, that John Wayne had cancer and votes Republican, that Warren Beatty is promiscuous, that Elton John is bisexual. And although we know all these intimate details about them, we never have to worry about their using our toothbrush or hogging the bathroom. For those who don't depend on television for the ephemeral information bits coming through the air, we have the same information disseminated in magazines and in our daily papers. We can even go out and buy a Farrah Fawcett-Majors poster or a Muhammed Ali doll or a Rolls-Royce to feel closer to Mick Jagger or Nate Thurman.

If Ovid sat among those in the televised fame tableaux, we could gossip about Ovid as if he were a friend as we do about Ali and Burt Reynolds. We could all be smug about just why he turned that girl into a tree. We would know. We could even speculate about whether he liked peanuts. Or whether he would turn Billy Carter into a peanut plant in his soon-to-be-forthcoming novel.

Knowing this, and understanding the role of television in the fame age, probably Ovid would not *want* to pursue the fame he envisioned two thousand years ago. But because we know it, and accept it, and are continuously affected by it, we also know that televised fame is the product of something else entirely, something that started generations ago when larger-than-life images were first introduced on a wide screen and seemed to move about as if by their own accord. It is as true today as it was a decade or two ago that television fame, although insidious and powerful in its electronic omnipresence, still doesn't hold a candle to movie fame.

CHAPTER

Fame in Los Angeles

*Technique is concrete. I want to do
things that will last because they have
substance and quality, not some
affectation or style, because that's all
bullshit.*

—Robert De Niro

1

From Magic to Technique

In Los Angeles, the fame game is a quest for initiation to the Hollywood legend. The winners are the ones who seem to have a magic touch, a formula, a direct line to the American dream. The tactic of the fame game is to give the public what it wants, and the fame mode is called "star quality."

Hollywood provides several arenas for its many fame seekers—from the promoters of Charles Manson's recording career to the creators of "All in the Family." But its most prestigious statusphere, spread out for miles on either side of Sunset Boulevard, is the one that makes the movies. "New Hollywood," it calls itself.

Old Hollywood, as everyone insists, is dead. And, as independent producer Robert Evans assures us, "New York is dead. England is dead. Europe is dead. Only Hollywood lives."

It sounds like the name of a motion picture: HOLLY-WOOD LIVES. But because Hollywood defines itself in images on and off the screen, it is often difficult to discern the difference between art and life, between illusion and reality, between professionalism and self-indulgence, between what

149

the public wants and what Hollywood wants to sell. The only stable, visible, discernible activity in Hollywood is its yearly celebration of self-deception, the Academy Awards pageant.

The focus of the fame game in Hollywood is not a forward-looking, trend-setting thrust as in New York, but a retrospective urge: an attempt to locate something Old Hollywood had that has been lost, something largely remembered as a statusphere of glamour, hope, happiness, riches, and drama, controlled like a cluster of independent countries by the old bosses: Cohen, Goldwyn, Selznik, Thalberg, Mayer.

Motion pictures, by definition, began as an attempt to do the impossible—to combine two contradictory conditions. Motion is movement, vitality, a quality of life. And it is constant change. A picture is static, unchanging and frozen, a relic of the past. So motion pictures achieved both conditions simultaneously, and in a sense, overthrew the laws of nature.

Movie stars became the symbols of that triumph over nature. Traditional time and space were obliterated and contained. Images looked real; illusion became an end in itself. Motion pictures became the possibility of life captured forever. Audiences went to see them again and again; they watched the gods and goddesses, the stars, fall in love time and time again, die again and again, perform acts of heroism and villainy over and over, never aging, always the same. Motion pictures made it seem possible to stay young forever, to stay alive forever. Even after actors and actresses died, the audience could watch them moving, and feel they were alive. Movies were bigger and were certainly more impressive and intense than life itself.

It was no accident that the famous in the Hollywood fame arena came to be called stars—celestial bodies orbiting high above a planet of workaday folk who looked to them for an image that was similar to legendary images of other eras, other times. These stars acted as we would have acted if we had not been so mortal, not so plain, not so mundane—and we strove to measure up to that image in our own lives, imitating gestures, mannerisms, costumes, fantasies.

And so the human beings who appeared on the screen were embued with "star quality"—linked as they were to the heavens and immortality. They led their audience to believe that if only they too were stars, they could break through the laws of nature.

No wonder, then, that every twenty years Hollywood produces a film called "A Star Is Born." Its motion tells the story of one star falling and another rising; and it offers hope to the audience that there is a chance for everyone; as soon as a big star falls there will be a vacant slot for us. If each generation watches the same film over and over or remakes of the same film over and over, what we see repeated becomes more real than what we experience directly. We begin to have new expectations—about ourselves mostly, but also (sometimes more intensely) about the stars.

The founders of the American motion picture industry at first had no idea that those moments in darkened theaters would so change the lives of their customers.

Hollywood in those days knew it was a dream factory. It produced war pictures, musical extravaganzas, sophisticated comedies, love stores, tear jerkers, westerns, adventures, cliff hangers, horror pictures, whodunits, and success stories by the score, making a lot of money and patting itself on the back because it was giving the public what they wanted—romance, comedy, entertainment, adventure, heroism, success. And what the public wanted most, Hollywood knew, was to believe again in the traditional American dream, the belief that all it takes to become rich and famous, to make anything possible, are hard work, patience, and hope.

Watching this on the screen, America fell in love with its

151

own dream again and again, and turned from the squalor of the Great Depression and the horrors of World War II to be reassured and entertained by the glitter and comedy and romance and drama of Fred Astaire and Ginger Rogers, Dick Powell and Ruby Keeler, Jimmy Cagney and Joan Blondell, Mickey Rooney and Judy Garland, William Powell and Jean Harlow, Greer Garson and Ronald Coleman, Humphrey Bogart and Mary Astor, Frederick March and Myrna Loy, James Stewart and Jean Arthur, John Wayne and Maureen O'Hara, Spencer Tracy and Katharine Hepburn, Cary Grant and Ingrid Bergman, W.C. Fields and Mae West, Robert Taylor and Greta Garbo, Clark Gable and Vivien Leigh.

So Hollywood with its elegance and splendor, its massive studios, its glamorous stars under long contracts, its elaborate costumes and storybook castles, bought the very dream it was merchandising. Its famous producers, famous writers, and famous stars came to Hollywood with a pioneering spirit, hoping to fulfill the dream for themselves and for posterity. They worked hard and long hours, forging a cinematic art that had never been imagined before, believing all along that in Hollywood, everything was new and everything was possible. The possibilities seemed to work: the new medium of motion pictures captured the hearts of America and made the makers rich and famous—and in the end, legendary. Their idea of pioneering in the new medium produced ingeniously creative technical wonders on the screen that still astonish the movie makers today. But most of all, the successful producers and writers and stars of Hollywood seemed to have something beyond star quality or technical brilliance that astonished even them. Magic, it was called.

Garbo had it, and Gable, and Hepburn, and Tracy, and Bogart, and Bette Davis—a magical presence or aura that brought them beyond stardom to become legends in their own time. Vague and undefined as it was, something magical happened when Cary Grant and Ingrid Bergman kissed on the steps of the wine cellar in "Notorious," and it happened again when John Wayne threw Maureen O'Hara on the bed in "The Quiet Man." Every time Hepburn and Tracy, or Bogart and Bacall, or Astaire and Rogers appeared on the screen it happened again—and again and again and again, filling each darkened theater with a magical atmosphere that flooded the sensations, not just for the moments that the movie was projected on a screen, but for hours and days and years later, sometimes for a lifetime.

Of course the studio bosses in Hollywood used their publicity mills to insure the public that merchandising magic was good for the country and that by feeding the dreams of America, the entertainment industry was performing a public service. They liked to say that their movies helped the American dream come true by encouraging American youth to work hard, to have hope, to strive to achieve new successes. And the youth of America, weaned on movies, took the dreams they saw literally. Some of them, in fact, grew up and moved West to capture the dream for themselves.

Selznik, Gable, Mayer, Thalberg, Harlow, Goldwyn, Chaplin had come to Hollywood to pursue the old American dream of pioneering and making money. They knew the difference between who they were and the work they did. But their successors, like Nicholson, Beatty, and Streisand, came to Hollywood not as pioneers but as people who had grown up watching the movies, wishing every day of their lives they could be like one of those people, bigger than life, worthy of public attention, with the right to fame and fortune and the chance to perform. The dream that drew people to New Hollywood was not a dream of succeeding at something new so much as a fantasy of blending into the promised land, of becoming part of one of the star statuspheres, a leading man or a leading lady, a big image, a famous image. So, determined to make themselves be as visibly happy as the old stars seemed, they tried to make the dream come true.

Today in New Hollywood, the need to believe in magic

153

and star quality and glamour and riches is still alive for both the industry and the audience, but since studios have disbanded and back lots no longer form the settings, the whole world has become a location site, making the famous seem more accessible and therefore less magical. At the same time, progress in achieving technical wonders on the screen has leaped ahead of artistic control to make such movies as "Jaws," "The Exorcist," "King Kong II," "Earthquake," and "Black Sunday" as technically wondrous as they are artistically boring. Yet these movies continue to pay the rent in New Hollywood: as producer Robert Evans is fond of saying, "the new art form in Hollywood is the blockbuster," which is to say that the old magic of Old Hollywood has now been replaced by technique. And while fame is still sought as the reward for that elusive element called star quality, the winners are not so inspired or inspiring as they were in the old days. While some stars in New Hollywood seem to have the magic (Streisand, Dunaway, Minnelli, Nicholson, Redford), today's audience is hard put to find a true equivalent of the Hepburns or Bergmans or Bogarts or Grants of yesterday.

Yet since every single one of the New Hollywood seekers was born into that same audience, everyone still carries that nagging memory around, and many have concluded that the public doesn't want anything new, just remakes of something that pleased them before. So we get a rash of remakes: "King Kong," "A Star Is Born," "African Queen," and no doubt coming soon, "Casablanca." Such genre films as "Airport," John Wayne westerns, and Charles Bronson plot-rehacks project onto the public a sense of disappointment the New Hollywood producers feel themselves—disappointment that they are not so creative, not so pioneering as their Hollywood forbears. Instead of looking more closely at the public to find real stories about real people that are new and true and alive, they draw back, figuring that since movie attendance has fallen off of late, the public has rejected them. Very few fame figures in Hollywood have actual contact with the American people, though most of them originally came from far less glamorous towns than New Hollywood. They don't go home to visit very often, claiming the trips are too depressing, reminding them of what they came west to forget. So the film industry looks to its predecessors for the answer. "Get me a 'Casablanca' for the seventies, and I'll pay through the nose for it," vows Robert Evans, and he means it.

But the difference between the current entertainment makers and their Old Hollywood models is only cosmetic. They believe in themselves and in the importance of what they do with a fervency at least as intense as that of a Goldwyn or a Mayer; and their belief renders their look and act merely ornamental. In spite of token blasphemies against their own industry, they work like crazy for the public good, but more specifically, for the sakes of their own fantasies. The figurehead of their belief is not a god, but the traditional American dream with all its magical possibilities. But now the magic seems to have vanished. So the stars of New Hollywood devote their waking hours to a communal effort to recapture the magic, and, knowing that nostalgia for the Old Hollywood is box office, they throw themselves into their remakes with obsessive dedication. When "A Star Is Born" was in production, bogging down, changing staffs, Barbra Streisand and Jon Peters sustained their desperation and justified their ambition by believing and repeating over and over like a mantra, "The whole world is waiting to hear our story."

Critics and co-workers and the public often confuse the performer with the character he or she is portraying. But in the case of "A Star Is Born," such similarities and ambiguities seemed almost deliberately indulged in—ostensibly for the sake of the audience, but more than likely for the sake of Streisand and Peters as well. Their urge was to let life blend into art. "People are curious. They want to know about us. That's what they come to see," said Streisand.

The studio executives saw another angle. They simply

155

instructed director Frank Pierson, "Shoot Streisand singing six numbers, and we'll make sixty million. We'd like it to be good, and that's what we hope you'll do, but if we have no choice . . ."

Pierson, after dangling in the middle of it all, after he'd finished making "A Star Is Born," wrote an article for *New West* magazine, placing the blame for the weaknesses of the film on the confusion created by Streisand and Peters between their private problems and the problems of the film. Pierson acted as his own mediacrat, absolving himself of all responsibility—a handy way of cleaning up after himself. Of Streisand's motives for producing the film, Pierson wrote: "If you think the film is you, if it is your effort to transform your lover into a producer worthy of a superstar, if you think it is a home movie about your love and your hope and your deepest feelings, if it's your life that you laid out for the folks and they don't smile back, that's death."

"Death" may be pushing it, but Pierson's pronouncement is a widely accepted one in the New Hollywood fame game: in an arena where magic has been replaced by technique, and where originality and creativity have been replaced by imitations of the old hits, so, too, has the pioneering spirit of Old Hollywood been replaced by a self-indulgent, love-me-love-my-film attitude in New Hollywood. It is as if Pierson gave a warning to Streisand: let it show, in spite of your hubris, how desperate you are for acceptance and success, and you risk not only falling on your face in public, but letting the whole world know that it hurt.

Yet in spite of its artistic failures, "A Star Is Born" was a box-office success. And Streisand, in spite of the fact that almost everyone who works with her says that she is one of the most difficult people to work with, is the only woman who can be called an official New Hollywood superstar. She possesses the magic of Harlow or Garbo. But as executive producer of her own star vehicle, she lost her magic and descended to the level of everybody else in New Hollywood, reflecting their ambition to hit it big with the safe, highly publicized blockbuster remake.

So what used to be artistic inspiration in Hollywood has now been replaced by commercialism and self-indulgence. Instead of giving the public what it wants—Old Hollywood's formula—the producers today offer what *they* want the public to want. So Robert Altman makes a film out of his dreams ("Three Women"), Peter Bogdanovitch tries to re-make slapstick comedy in his own vision ("What's Up, Doc"), and Peter Fonda stars in a movie that makes his real-life failures seem heroic ("Easy Rider"). Even Dino De Laurentiis, rather than admitting the simple truth that the time had come for a remake of "King Kong," likes to say that the idea for that imitation came to him when he walked into his daughter's bedroom and noticed a poster on her wall from the original 1933 version of the film. As De Laurentiis predicted in *Time* magazine,

> No one cry when "Jaws" die. But when the monkey die, people gonna cry. Intellectuals gonna love Kong; even film buffs who love the first Kong gonna love ours. Why? Because I no give them crap. I no spend two, three million to do quick business. I spend 24 million on my Kong. I give them quality. I got here a great love story, a great adventure. And she rated PG . . . for everybody!

To understand the leaps of logic and feeling that allow a man to talk that way about love and crap and quality is to understand the fame game in New Hollywood. Take the old classic film, make it technically more opulent than it was before, add what seems to be your own personal dedication to the project, and *voilà*: instant blockbuster and personal fame to boot. If they love my Kong they gonna love me, too, De Laurentiis seems to say.

David O. Selznik understood the power of publicity as well as De Laurentiis; but he used it for promotion, not for personal fame. He made a huge show of his search for the

157

right actress to play Scarlett O'Hara, testing nearly every major starlet in town for the role. The campaign he waged was enormous. At the premiere in Atlanta, he announced to the crowd: "This movie is for the people of Atlanta. If it pleases you, then I consider it a success."

They liked it; he considered the film a success, and he considered himself a success. He never asked them to like *him*. He saw the difference between power and fame and he chose power. His successors, like De Laurentiis, are trying for both fame and power, annoyed that power doesn't make them popular. They deliberately confuse business with self-indulgence and, perhaps inadvertently, in trying to claim the magic for themselves, seize it away from the public. When Robert Evans on national television announces to Mike Douglas, "For me, the real stars are the writers. I would rather have a Robert Towne on my next four films than a Robert Redford," he announces that for him, Redford is a shadowy figure on a screen. The real star of the film is the man who puts together the actors, workers, and sets, he implies: myself.

The talk show audience, on the other hand, doesn't know who Towne is. We serve only as a mirror for Evans, reflecting the insult back to Redford. But Evans, super-mogul though he is, is an ineffectual star. He mistakenly thinks his behind-the-scenes power will touch the audience. The audience is bored by him. We want Redford.

Robert Evans epitomizes the relationship between the winners of Old Hollywood's fame game and the losers of today. On a business trip to Hollywood in 1955, Evans got himself discovered at the Beverly Hills Hotel by Norma Shearer, who thought he was a dead ringer for Irving Thalberg and arranged for him to portray the legendary producer in "Man of a Thousand Faces." Instead of becoming an Oscar-winning actor, however, Evans remained a businessman, eventually slipping into the fame slot of producer. But in spite of his eventual rise to the position of head of production at Paramount and then his lesser but still highly visible role as an independent producer, he is not satisfied. "You never get thanked," he complains. "Francis Ford Coppola thanked everyone else involved in the success of 'The Godfather' at the Academy Awards ceremony but me. And then, when 'Godfather II' won, he forgot to thank me again." The very next year, Evans arranged for a retrospective showing of films he had acted in as well as produced. He began giving interviews to mediacrats, talking about his feelings, his failed marriages, his sense of despair and his exhaustion. "I realize now that no woman could love a man like I've turned into," he told talk-show host Mike Douglas; and it is hard to believe that such a master of image manipulation is unaware of the seductive effect of his fame pose. Six months later, he married fame winner Phyllis George, mediacrat and former Miss America.

Evans is at once New Hollywood's spokesman and its pariah, according to one film reviewer. He is good copy because he is a professional. He still reads *Women's Wear Daily* every day. He has taken credit for movies he didn't produce—but he has his act together, and he's appealing. "I'm not rich," he tells reporters, as if they are his intimates; "but I live as if I'm very, very rich." He flaunts his personal life, mixing power with innocence, distracting his audience from ambition and fame greed, turning private experience into an art form, hugging and kissing his new bride for photographers. Evans works eighteen hours a day, and he says he's really looking for a good and true love story to produce, that making movies is more erotic to him than real life: "One of the greatest comes of my life is to look at a picture forming." For someone like Evans, success is attained when there are no divisions between life and work and art; the private self fades into the public image.

Warren Beatty is a bigger winner than Evans because he has managed to succeed in almost every Hollywood fame role. After he established himself as a "quality" actor and

159

not just Shirley MacLaine's brother, he produced and starred in the highly successful "Bonnie and Clyde." After that double victory, his next big step in the fame game was to write, produce, and star in "Shampoo," using his cultivated playboy image to promote the film. Beatty appeared on the "Today Show" and pleaded earnestly with Barbara Walters, "But don't you see—promiscuous people feel pain, too!"

Beatty's strategy was first to establish that he had old-fashioned star quality. Then he took that star quality and exploited it in the New Hollywood tradition of producer as well. By the time he was promoting "Shampoo," he was able to mix all the roles at once. He deliberately mistook his fame power for personal authenticity and asked the public to laud his personal pain as well as his public narcissism. And it worked.

The difference in quality between "Bonnie and Clyde" and "Shampoo"—artistically, morally, creatively—is absorbed as an irrelevancy in Beatty's various victories within the fame game. To the extent that his local and national audience confuse the hairdresser's plight with Beatty's plight, he is a Big Fame Winner. His triumph derives from his skills as a public narcissist, distracting from the fact that in New Hollywood, as in Old Hollywood, power and money are the big prizes of the fame game. And the greatest coup of all is that he can still be seductive, still play hard to get, still talk to the press only when he chooses to, still project his privacy only through the vehicles he chooses to invent. Sure, he walks through the Beverly Wilshire lobby now and then: he has to in order to get home. Beatty denies he has deliberately chosen a public residence because he must have an audience to keep on playing.

If they run out of remakes and are uninspired by personal obsessions, studio heads also look to computer polls to discover what the public wants. Professional pulse takers complement the instincts of the bosses, measuring responses at controlled public screenings by processing laugh levels and tension levels and questionnaires. When the marketing machine predicted that "Lucky Lady" would be a hit, the studio head responded by saying, "Get me Liza Minnelli, get me Burt Reynolds, get me Gene Hackman!" Hackman resisted but the producer said, "I don't care what he costs. Get me Hackman!" And Hackman eventually succumbed at $1.25 million. Agent Sue Mengers defended her client: "I mean it wasn't exactly as though he was being asked to exterminate people. The studio executives came up with the kind of money that made it almost obscene for him not to do the film."

The crude and greedy fame pose of New Hollywood, as flaunted by superagent Sue Mengers, is based on the notion that nothing matters but clout and box office, that the old elegance, the ambiance of dignity and *noblesse oblige* which nurtured the glamour of Noel Coward, Douglas Fairbanks, Jr., Greta Garbo, and Mary Pickford is dead; that everyone in New Hollywood is desperate, and under the surface shine lies bald, tasteless ambition.

Naturally, then, some of the stars of the caliber of Old Hollywood drop out of the fame game once they have won. As Marlon Brando recently told a *Time* reporter, "I notice that the width of a Hollywood smile in my direction is commensurate with how much my last picture grossed. Acting," he went on to say, "is an empty and useless profession. I do it for the money, because for me there is no pleasure."

Elizabeth Taylor, another of the few remaining vintage stars, moved away to Washington and a new husband. And veteran film director Laslo Benedek ("Death of a Salesman," "The Wild One") said, "When Bob Evans declared the new Hollywood art form the blockbuster, I decided to take the job as head of the film graduate school of New York University."

For the ones who stay, the real trick is to make fame worth the trouble, to nurse the dream that they will be transformed

161

by manipulating images. The chance for official transformation does not take place on a screen or in an office or at poolside or in the mirror, but that one spring night at the Academy Awards pagent when the audience is watching but not present. It is not the films they gather to celebrate, not the achievements, but the magic of the chance for a permanent acknowledgment of eternal fame.

2

The Academy Awards

The outdoor bleachers fill. Technicians huddle in front, cordoning off two paths on the sidewalk in front of the Dorothy Chandler Pavilion. One path, for the 3,000 guests with tickets, leads right to the doors of the Pavilion. The other, for the face-famous, leads onto a wooden pedestal where columnist and professional greeter Army Archerd will stand, waiting for them as one by one they walk up, talk through his microphone to the crowd and, through the television cameras, to the folks back home.

"I do this every year," a quiet man who sits by himself in the upper left hand corner of the bleachers says softly. "I believe in coming just to see what goes on. I don't bother them. I don't ask for autographs. I just like knowing the thing is still alive. I used to come with my wife, but she passed away a year ago last October. This is my second time alone."

Evening settles around the bleachers and very expensive automobiles begin to snarl up traffic in a circle all around the Pavilion, honking at each other in spite of the specially uniformed traffic directors who lead the ones with yellow and red cards on their windshields to their designated garages. Those with gold cards will drive right up to the curb where they will drop off the honored guests. Each honored guest will be met by a monitor who will send word by

163

walkie-talkie to Army Archerd so he knows who is coming next.

By the time the festivities begin, the people in the bleachers feel as though they belong there in a special way because they arrived first. They are neither members of the Academy of Motion Picture Arts and Sciences nor members of the press corps. They will not go inside the Pavilion where the awards take place. But they are crucial participants. They have, in a sense, created this fame tabloid. Or perhaps they merely buy it. But for them, it is a revival meeting, a religious ritual; and they take pride in the purity of their motives. They scream with all their might when Elizabeth Taylor appears on the arm of George Cukor, her official escort, with dress designer Halston a few paces behind them, and walks up to the pedestal to tell Army and through Army to tell them how she feels, how she felt the first time she was nominated, how she felt when she won, how much the Academy Awards mean to her. "I *am* the Awards," she replies.

Then she is helped back down to pose on the cordoned-off path for the *paparazzi*. She sends a special kiss over the heads of the press corps to the bleachers, then disappears inside for the ceremony.

Since there is grave concern in Hollywood that the magic of Old Hollywood has been lost, the new community of technicians responds to this concern by making a yearly attempt to recapture the magic. So every spring, the traditional season of rebirth, the movie fraternity get all dressed up and gather to celebrate their own rite of passage, to pay homage to the magic, to try to keep it alive.

It's a televised ritual—the fame game televised, but not in the same way as the Johnny Carson Show. Here the famous (in fact, all those who will see the ceremony from inside the Pavilion) are outsiders. The only ones who really belong are the fans cheering in the stands, locked outside. They are the true believers. For them the old magic *is* still alive.

164

And yet seventy million Americans—more of us than voted in the last national election—watch the ceremony at home on television, willing to sit through the tedious speeches, commercials and all, through technical awards we don't even care about; and by the time the Awards for Best Actor and Actress are announced, we are in as much of a frenzy as the nominees.

Jack Nicholson, nominee for best actor, ushers his companion, Anjelica Huston, down the aisle. Once seated, he fidgets. He takes his sunglasses from his tuxedo pocket, studies himself in their lenses for a moment, then puts them on. He punches the man to his right on the shoulder. Then he leans forward and concentrates on his knuckles.

One of the ABC ushers says to his partner, "God, Nicholson is wearing sunglasses again this year. He must be scared we'll see how strung-out he is."

"Bullshit," says the partner. "Sunglasses are part of the Old Hollywood bit. He probably thinks they make him a star."

Charlton Heston appears. Nicholson cracks his knuckles, looking both proud to be in the company of big fame winners and uncomfortable at being exposed. Like Sylvester Stallone who will come next year hoping for initiation, like the series of potential "best actors" before him, Nicholson sits and waits. The years of the Oscars blend one into the other.

In less than two hours, Nicholson will learn whether or not he has pleased his peers in the industry. Agents, the press, the competition, the name-famous, face-famous, job-famous, family-famous are all somewhere watching to learn whether or not he, Jack Nicholson, will at last after four nominations win the coveted Oscar. The gold, man-shaped trophy can transform him from an actor who works, as he has said, "because acting is a way of getting pressure off yourself," into a legend in his own time. A winner.

Inside the Dorothy Chandler Pavilion, the crowd leans forward to see Elizabeth Taylor walk down the aisle, much

165

smaller than her screen image. In her seat as she arranges her
scarlet Halston, a look of dead seriousness comes over her.
Maybe she is concentrating hard on the lines she will read
when her turn comes. Maybe she can hear the couple behind
her whispering, "She sure isn't what she used to be," in a
tone that sounds as though she's betrayed them.

Nicholson fidgets and waits. The Academy Awards ceremony appears to celebrate the stars like him, but in fact, by
placing them in the audience, it reminds them who isn't boss.
They are among the least powerful players in the fame game.
So they wait, knowing that tonight offers something other
than power for them, something that might be called a
salvation of the actor's fantasy. For this is a ceremony of
transformation from obscurity to stardom. In it, the actor is
elevated to a peculiarly American version of immortality:
once he wins, he will always be an Oscar winner, his movie
will always be shown and reshown, and no matter how
unsuccessful he may be after tonight's ceremony, he will
always be remembered for his Oscar-winning performance,
his big moment of fame. Someone else may have the power
to direct his career, but long after that power has dissipated,
his fame will live on.

Backstage it is clear that the festival is serious business.
There is no personal touching, only cheek-kissing and si-
lence. Mirrors and agents are consulted. One year when
three old-fashioned superstars are invited to appear—Hepburn, Streisand, and Taylor—they slip through the wings
when their turn comes, and they ignore each other. Candice
Bergen introduces herself to the hugely powerful survivor,
Lew Wasserman. Katharine Hepburn—the year she deigns to
appear—demands one of the two backstage dressing rooms
exclusively for herself; and her proper British constant
companion, Phyllis Wilbourne, has had it sanitized from top
to bottom. Hepburn knows she has been invited as an Old
Hollywood throwback and she plays her part with the old-
fashioned arrogance of royalty. There are perfunctory

smiles for the occasional camera or mediacrat. No time for small talk; this is the big time.

As the cameras pan, we at home get ready for the presentation of the awards and the nominees close up look nervous. Are they really nervous? Are they acting? Are they performers? Immortals? Members of the audience? Will he crack? Will she win? Will he be gracious if he loses? Is she human? Is he mortal?

Constant closeups of the actors in the audience—aging, competitive, vulnerable, scared—are set up by the Academy to give us a peek at the real people behind the images. Only so long as the stars cooperate to sustain the industry's myth of fame philanthropy will the industry support them. The communal ritual set up in the tradition of ageless springtime fertility rites—to rekindle the belief in perpetual rebirth— every year reflects more and more the desperate need to win, to be accepted, to be famous.

Because the power of fame is so illusory and fragile and so subject to the ravages of time, in these moments of public exposure, all the stars' fears come close to the surface. All the frailties they meant to leave at home threaten to show at any moment. But if an actor can be transformed into a legend in his or her own time while the whole world is watching, human frailties become irrelevant forever. The whole purpose of Hollywood fame is to distract from those frailties by rekindling a belief in the version of immortality promoted and tentatively maintained by the motion picture industry. The fame-seekers who win are the ones who are elevated to ageless fame. The power-seekers who win are the ones who can control ageless images, sustaining the confusion between the process of life and the process of business that keeps Hollywood alive.

A huge screen is unrolled. The gates of Pickfair—the palace Mary Pickford and her husband Douglas Fairbanks, built years and years before — open and cameras take everybody in America onto the ultra-private grounds, into

167

the lush, formal gardens, through the big front door, as Walter Mirisch, president of the Academy, explains that America's Sweetheart had wanted to appear in person tonight but was not feeling well. Instead, we accompany Mirisch by videotape into her salon and see an immobile, fluttery, birdlike old woman, a parody of immortality, on a backdrop of pink satin.

In the dialogue that follows, Mirisch and Pickford manage to expose all the hidden realities Hollywood's images keep from itself and the world. Smack in the middle of the Dorothy Chandler Pavilion, projected on a twenty-foot screen, televised into the living rooms of seventy million people who have tuned in for their yearly glimpse of Hollywood magic, is the unspoken truth that belies Hollywood's promise of immortality. For the projection of America's dying sweetheart confirms the fact that *she* is the future of every fame winner, fame seeker, and fame lover in the world.

So Hollywood's crowning ceremony, billed as the moment of immortality for its big fame winners, carries with it a fame truth so deeply disappointing that no one really wins. Those who are awarded the Oscar and the promise of a place in film history have also seen Pickfair, and know that their moment of immortality is just that, a moment. Beneath the pageantry, then, the Academy Awards is not an apotheosis: it is at best a walk-on, the heralding of the beginning of a decline, a statement of replaceability. No wonder it seems impossible for even accomplished actors to walk gracefully away from the podium: it is as if the Award has given them a blessing of empty salvation—"You were lost but now you are found; you have become your image; you can rest assured now that *you are your act*. And your act is all that counts."

After the blessing, each winner is taken up on a backstage elevator to the press room to share his victory with posterity.

George Burns, after he wins the Best Supporting Actor award, is asked by the pressroom hecklers how he feels about taking his late friend Jack Benny's role in "The Sunshine Boys."

"Well," he says, "I thought about Jack at the time I was offered the role and I thought it was sad, I felt bad about it— but life has to go on, and I did the job."

Then the reporter asks, "Did you think about it tonight?"

And George Burns, irritated but too much of a pro to let it show, throws the question back at the questioner by answering, "Well, no, I hadn't thought about it, but I'm thinking about it now."

Wherever mortality rears its head, the Academy of Motion Picture Arts and Sciences gives it another name, emphasizing the permanence of the Oscars. But in spite of director Billy Friedkin's instructions to the contrary, when the recently deceased Peter Finch wins the award for Best Actor, his widow, Eletha, is invited to the podium by Paddy Chayevsky. Apparently overwhelmed by the victory and the grief, her presence has a gushing intensity that cuts through the conventional theatrics and causes squirming backstage and among the viewers. Like Mary Pickford's or Charlie Chaplin's aging frailty, like Louise Fletcher's deaf-and-dumb hand language in 1976, such moments proclaim the human side of Hollywood, the truths about fame that are traditionally ignored.

So the Academy Awards' promise to immortalize stars is really a show for the fans in the bleachers and the viewers in their living rooms back home. But the audience inside the Pavilion that night is hit hard year after year by the fact that Hollywood can manipulate images of their lives and of their films for eternity, but it cannot keep them alive forever.

The stars—some of them openly—resent being put through the paces of a ritual which, like marriage and baptism, seems to be becoming extinct. And giving the ultimate honor to Peter Finch, *a dead man,* is disconcerting to everyone. The film clip from "Network" shows Finch's character at his most agonized, crying out in despair. The mediacrats in the

169

pressroom speculate to each other about what it all means.

"Maybe that's what killed him," ponders one columnist.

"No, it wasn't that, it was the publicity tour. They just ran him ragged."

"You're both wrong," says a third. "It was that wife of his."

At the same moment, that year's Best Actress, apotheosized for an instant for playing a role, looks at her Oscar and smirks. At the moment when Nicholson or Holden or Dunaway or Streisand first touches the man-shaped trophy, he or she touches its eternity and knows it. "Eat your heart out, America," says the smile of the winner, now officially blessed by star quality, still powerless and mortal, but, for this moment at least, more famous than anyone on earth.

The film community gathers together every Spring for the sole purpose of holding onto hope. To live as performer and audience at once, to celebrate the magic transformation of human beings—with private flaws and fears and worries—into public legends, is Hollywood's attempt to fulfill the American dream. It is still a dream to have it both ways—technically and magically. It is still a dream of overthrowing nature. As long as the dream persists, as long as it can manage its spectacular blur between fame and power, magic and technique, death and immortality, and as long as the public believes in it, Hollywood lives.

3

Marketing the American Dream

There are still hordes of people making pilgrimages to Hollywood to make it big as screenwriters, producers, directors, actors—or simply to join the public narcissism—in spite of the warnings that the only chance for newcomers in Hollywood is in television and television is always garbage, and that movies have lost imagination and originality and have no room for new blood.

So ex-television stars like Barry Newman leave the television medium that once announced every week, "Barry Newman *is* Petrocelli." "Barry Newman is me, not Petrocelli," he protests. "I want to sing, I want to be in films," he insists, furious at the limitations that the character he portrayed imposed on his ambition, willing to risk obscurity for the sake of the old dream. "Look, television makes you smaller than the audience; in movies, you're bigger than the audience, and that's what I want." But he has yet to upstage Petrocelli.

Ironically, television has surpassed motion pictures by providing old-fashioned stars, completely defined and promoted as characters, not as human beings. Telly Savalas is popular because for his fans he *is* Kojak. Henry Winkler appears on children's tee-shirts because for them he *is* the

Fonz. Of course, Winkler, now that he is no longer a fame-seeker, is unwilling to equate himself with the image of the Fonz. But television transmits Winkler as the Fonz again and again, just as Old Hollywood transmitted images on a movie screen again and again. So the public buys the new magic and wears tee-shirts that show a likeness of the Fonz, just as they went without undershirts so they could link themselves to the magic of Clark Gable.

But manipulating mythic images and selling them to the public is still the sleight-of-hand specialty of the motion picture industry. As enchantment becomes entertainment, entertainment becomes big business. The trick in the business is seducing the audience into believing that what we get is what we want. And the biggest fame winners understand the techniques if not the mystery of transforming flesh and blood into star quality. Although Henry Winkler and Sylvester Stallone started out in show business in the same movie, "The Lords of Flatbush," it is Stallone who, because he stuck with movies rather than television, and because he fought his way through New Hollywood's bureaucracy to maintain control of his own star vehicle, leaped beyond the Fonz's trendy stardom to immortalize himself as Rocky. But Stallone didn't stop there: he went on to write himself into the highly publicized story-behind-the-movie by showing how he, Stallone, had succeeded in real life just as Rocky had succeeded in the movie—by going the distance, by overcoming enormous odds, by fighting and winning where others had failed. By obliterating the difference between himself and Rocky, Stallone won the loyalty and admiration of his audience, then moved onto an even higher fame plateau by convincing them not that Stallone was Rocky (less a person than an image), but that Rocky was Stallone (a real person and an instant myth).

Because they live in the entertainment capital of the world, because they live in the center of the American myth machine, New Hollywood people feel exposed, constantly looked at both on screen and in private life, by people who have seen them or heard of them and want to know what they are really like. So they are always perceived as performing. No wonder they hide out: Warren Beatty finally left the Beverly Wilshire to isolate himself in a classic mountain-top hideaway mansion; Brando, George C. Scott, Hepburn, Pacino, and others epitomize the elusive, publicity-shy fame winners who pretend a pose of fame innocence. It is easy for an observer to mistake the public performances of New Hollywood actors for the seemingly genuine glamour and pleasures of their predecessors. They also seem to *work* just as hard, mixing private goals with public performance, just as in the old days. For example, when he was publicizing the film, "The Shoes of the Fisherman," Anthony Quinn told the mediacrats that when he was working on the role of the Pope, he was unable to sleep with his wife. It was his way of getting into the part. Similarly, Robert Evans, in promoting "Marathon Man," claimed that Dustin Hoffman stayed up for four days and four nights just so he would be authentically exhausted when he was required to *act* exhausted.

Self-denial for the sake of a movie role sounds like the classic drive for artistic excellence, as though the primary motive of an actor is to give a performance of the highest quality. But by giving the audience a peek at the behind-the-scenes work of real people, Quinn and Evans simply primed the market. So even self-denial in Hollywood, like scandal and tragedy, becomes grist for the publicists' mill no matter what the original motive. The message is: These superstars may be rewarded way out of porportion, but they pay for what they earn. But the actual fact of it is: These superstars (or their agents) know how to milk the audience by blending private and public life.

Such confusion is also deliberate on the part of New Hollywood's powerful elite. "I don't know what works," says agent Sue Mengers. "I just know what doesn't work." The actors she supplies draw over a million dollars per picture. "I must be doing something right," she wagers behind the scenes. The powers of New Hollywood know exactly what they're doing, but they aren't telling: they're mimicking the coy innocence of their Old Hollywood idols.

If Old Hollywood employed full-time publicists to keep stars' images slick, in New Hollywood, stardom means not being the star but managing the images. So Streisand, Newman, Beatty, Poitier, Redford have recognized—like Pickford and Chaplin and Fairbanks—the potential business power behind the images, and founded their own production companies.

They are imitating if not calling the bluff of producers like Evans and De Laurentiis, who use acting techniques to pretend they're in the fame game for more than power and money. Superstars take on other roles than acting to make up for the fact that actors hold less and less exclusive power. John Cassavetes, Warren Beatty act as directors as well, bankrolling their productions in part with their acting earnings.

Thus the power of stardom has been officially stretched into technical manipulation. Today's stars do not want to settle for the hollow and transitory fame of Old Hollywood—they want to control their own images, their own audiences, their own profits. It is not enough for them to give the public what it wants; like their counterparts elsewhere—the politicians in Washington and the trend-setters in New York—the new fame-seekers of Hollywood want to make a difference, to go down in history. This is why De Laurentiis and Streisand and Stallone each made an enormous effort to convince the public that *their* movie (even "Rocky" was basically a remake of the generic boxing film) would outstrip its classic predecessor, would be remembered long after the original was forgotten, would become a "new" classic. From their point of view it was not fame they were after, but rather the money, prestige, and blockbuster image that would place them in cinematic history as important filmmakers, people

174

of greater substance and clout than the other, less powerful stars.

But while the official goal in New Hollywood is to manipulate star quality into profitable images, the unofficial goal is to *feel* like a star, to make the difference between the dreams of youth and the reality of adulthood disappear. For the truly famous who have dismissed the old glamour as hollow and passé, that's the magic of New Hollywood, that's the goal. And it is a difficult, if not impossible, goal to achieve.

Two kinds of technique are being employed by Hollywood's fame-seekers as short-cuts to the magic: psychotherapy as a means to star quality, and (as we have seen) cinematographic spectacle as a substitute for creativity. But even science has trouble erasing contradictions. At the same time that therapists are training them to get in touch with themselves, their managers are telling them to get their acts together. So they try to have it both ways, getting together acts that make it look as if they *are* in touch with themselves. They procure their therapists for image-polishing, not for self-scrutiny.

And no wonder.

"Self-knowledge is always bad news," reads a sign in the office of United Artists' vice-president Marcia Nassiter. "It's hard to have a private life in this business," she says. "Everybody is always watching."

Marcia Nassiter is one of the few fame figures to acknowledge the personal side of the fame discrepancy: off camera the stars have human frailties and need help in looking good. So part of Hollywood's attraction for them is the promise of being transformed by the magic—transformed into "real" Hollywood people who are absorbed into the dream.

The best intentioned fame seekers in the industry may spend the morning at a massage or encounter group or hypnotherapist to find themselves, but when they walk into Nassiter's office to negotiate a deal, her sign makes it clear what's expected of them if they want to succeed at the fame game. In the movie business, illusion has a bigger payoff than reality.

Joanne Woodward, like Woody Allen, admits that all her life her biggest wish was to be someone else. Despite their substantial talent, these and other movie stars find it hard to celebrate themselves. So they put their self-dissatisfaction to work for them by literally becoming someone else. Hollywood offers the perfect excuse: their public wants them to be somebody else. They owe it to the patrons who have made them millionaires.

When men and women who have grown rich through the cultivation of their own image see bus tours go by their private homes, full of strangers craning their necks to find out what they're really like, they come to realize that they have grown rich by being what the public wants after all, and it's their job to continue to put on a good show. They remember the days when they sat in the audience, buying tickets to touch the magic. The drive to ignore the memories of those days in the audience is what gives them the energy to turn their real lives into images for sale. The audience is their mirror and in a way their enemy. A narcissist who doesn't like his image can't be fond of his reflection.

They *are* narcissists, people who are in love with their own images and try to change who they "really are" into how they ought to look. In New Hollywood, the purest reward of fame is the public narcissism—wanting to be the star you already are, and admiring yourself for it. This is easy to do in a place where huge billboards—larger than half a dozen movie screens glued together—line either side of the Sunset Strip, each one offering a gigantic painting of a rock star or movie star or nightclub star. The billboards are not really for the general public but for the people in the entertainment industry who ride in their carefully selected automobiles up and down Sunset Boulevard. Images loom over them as they make their way to and from their homes and their offices and the Polo Lounge in the Beverly Hills

176

Hotel, dealing as they drive, planning what they will wear to screenings and dinner parties, comparing their reflections in the rear-view mirror with the faces that smile down at them.

There is a restaurant called Hamburger Hamlet underneath the billboard at the Beverly Hills end of the Sunset Strip. The restaurant has a veranda that overlooks the street, and it has valet parking. It is common to see a Rolls Royce or an antique Mercedes pull up with custom license plates spelling the first or last name of the face-famous driver, who tosses the keys to an attendant and walks inside in clear view of the diners, acting as if he is completely unaware of them. Most patrons wear blue jeans and tee-shirts. You would think you were in the heart of the country if it weren't that the people were particularly slim and carefully placed. But the fact is that since the time of Mayer and Selznik, the fame-in-Hollywood pose has been modified to what some call a "natural" style. The idea is to wear make-up to look like one is wearing no make-up, underwear that looks like one is wearing no underwear, denims that cost more than flannels and are fitted and customed to resemble the denims of the workers back home (who, by the way, dress to resemble what their favorite movie stars wear). These human qualities seem to bring popularity, both in the local fame arena and at the box office, for when fans think they resemble the stars and the stars resemble them, they'll attend more movies where they can view their own images.

So the need to mesh private personality with public image repeats itself over and over again, all over Hollywood, and therefore the world, and if it seems that the old magic has truly been lost, that nothing is left in New Hollywood but layers of hype upon more hype, there are many who leap to the defense of those who are (some would say) forced to perform all the time.

Irene Kassorla, who refers to herself as "the most successful and highly paid therapist in this town," insists, "Famous people are very special and very different from the average

177

man. They're more intelligent, and they have a sensitivity. They can see things the average person can't see. In the way certain pigs are trained to sniff out the truffles and go right to them, famous people are like that. . . . Maybe under God we're all equal, but famous, talented people are special." And so Dr. Kassorla tells her famous patients what they want to hear; fame seekers find it easy to believe they have star quality.

Does Barbra Streisand feel she is masquerading? She makes a life with her hairdresser who makes her into a California beauty and helps keep her the number one female box office attraction. After a few mythical, manic hours with a therapist like Kassorla, she can be convinced she's blessed, she's been touched. "Go ahead, yell at me," she can say, "I know I'm a star, I'm famous." Which in this case means in part, "I've got power"—the power of pure fame, which brings a spectacular sense of confidence along with intense insecurity. "Part of our society kills what it loves, despises what it's created," Streisand said in an interview. "You've got to be destroyed, buried, pushed right back down again."

Why put up with such nonsense? Hollywood hypnotherapist John Kappas says of his famous patients, "It's the very insecurity of having been unacceptable—that's the opposite of famous from where they sit—that gives them the drive to work so hard to be star famous. The contradiction between what they were and what they are is so great that it thrusts them into actually living in their own image. The famous and seekers after fame take the neurosis and they make it work: they live inside their image." But sometimes the image cracks under pressure.

Laurence Olivier, while directing Marilyn Monroe in "The Prince and The Showgirl," at one point asked her to be sexy. On the verge of tears, she turned her face to the wall and said, "I don't know how," and had to leave the set. She could obviously *look* sexy, but to *be* sexy was too much, at least that day under those circumstances. In Hollywood, living up to the image on demand isn't always easy.

Image-keeping can also be difficult outside of a prescribed acting role. Olivier himself, in a recent interview for the *New York Times* says, "I've been terribly disappointed in myself and in my attitude toward the public. Yesterday, when I was approached by fans on the set, I sort of looked away, instead of saying, 'Oh, come my darlings, and let me give you my autograph.' When I was very young, I imagined myself at the top of the steps of the stage door saying, 'My people, come let me sign your books, you funny little people.' But the first time I ever faced a crowd, I just ran for dear life, terrified. It's funny to live my whole life facing the bastards and then I can't really face them when I see them face to face. Yesterday I kept saying to myself, 'Go ahead, smile at them.' But I always weary of starting something I don't know how to continue. After I smiled, what would I do next?"

Of course, Olivier's fame verges on imperial nobility, so he may find it tough to relate to commonplace Americans.

But perhaps the similarities between the famous and the commonplace are stronger than they look. John Kappas says, "Almost every actor or actress I've ever worked with, or any person who has reached tremendous heights of success, functions with a different personality with the public; and after a while he learns to carry that personality with him and he finds that he cannot feel comfortable out of that role, so he avoids the people who know him from the past."

For example, after Lana Turner and Artie Shaw were divorced, she told Shaw that she had been to bed with a man that afternoon who had paid her the highest compliment of all. He had said, "Just think of all the guys in America who want to be in my place!" Lana Turner could not resist telling her former husband that all over America there were men who loved her as she was meant to be loved: as a public image, without concerning themselves with who or what she was close up.

Marilyn Monroe's magic depended at least partly on her look of naked vulnerability and perhaps on a real inability or unwillingness to always live within her image. Walking unsteadily out of the hospital after having a miscarriage, she was engulfed by reporters and photographers. "Marilyn, we love you, how are you, how do you feel?" And with thousands of people around her, she averted her face, pleading with them to leave her alone. She had risked what Garbo refused to risk—total exposure. And she was stuck in public with her personal sense of failure at womanhood—having a baby. All she could show them was the truth—her powerlessness—when all they wanted to see was the image the public believed. Her image was her full-time job and her private failure became public failure.

The same truths held in the old days for Gable and Lombard and Tracy and Hepburn, but they had put in enough time before the instant fame of television made replaceability so painfully easy. They seemed larger than life to their public, in part because their bosses nurtured their personal images with the same skill and care with which they produced their films and, at the right times, hid them away.

But now the bosses want fame for themselves. And since in New Hollywood many of the actors are bosses and many of the bosses are actors, the only real winner in Hollywood's fame game is fame itself: personal fame that feeds on narcissism and profits by it as well; blind fame that transforms each player into a marketable image; popular fame that makes the audience want to see the stars' humanity but not their mortality. So the contradiction inherent to the American Dream—that hard work, hope, and patience can make anything possible—is that nothing is possible without fame, and that fame, even with its own, Old Hollywood rewards, is not power.

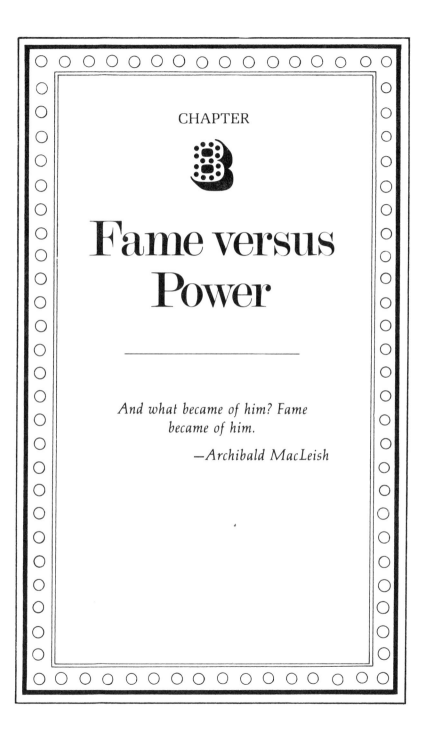

CHAPTER

3

Fame versus Power

And what became of him? Fame became of him.

—Archibald MacLeish

Fame attracts people who want attention and the accoutrements of power but not the responsibility of power itself. As we have seen, fame brings primarily narcissistic victories. Power, on the other hand, involves public control, the chance to get people to do what you want them to do. If all you want is for people to look at you, then stardom is power. But if you want to control what people want and what they buy and what they are allowed to do and not do, stardom is self-defeating, a coward's version of power. If you want acknowledgement of your magic, fame is your goal. But if you want deliberate manipulation, you want power.

To those without either, the main difference between fame and power is that fame is visible and power is not. So in every arena of fame there is a player who remains publicly invisible but is intensely recognized by the outsiders: the one who runs the show, the one with the muscle. Power, like vulnerability, is usually underplayed. Its implication is *you ain't seen nothing yet.* Even Michael Korda in his book *Power!* argues that power must never be flaunted. As Washingtonians know only too well, power must be hidden in order to work. So most network heads, newspaper tycoons, movie backers, directors of corporations—powers behind the fame game—usually keep out of the public fame arenas. Owning the machinery of fame is enough for them. They consider public appearance a sign of weakness, an indication that they may be losing their grip. They can afford a haughty disdain—like Salvador Dali when he was asked by an eager reporter if he had ever taken drugs. "Taken drugs?" Dali's famous moustache quivered. "I *am* drugs!" So the powers behind the fame rate themselves and each other by their ownership of the action, not by condescending to perform in public. Of course the carefully polished and protected image of aloof innocence, of modest effortlessness, still persists with the fame-free power achievers of this country who scorn fame-seeking as vulgarity and give actors and politicians a pose to imitate. As long as the social elite underplay their power, the rest of us can nurse the illusion that we live in a classless society.

But in our hunger for an elite with *noblesse oblige*, we've given our celebrities the veneer of power. Our fantasy is that they'll transform themselves into real nobility and take care of us. In 1976, even though he didn't want to run, Walter Cronkite was proclaimed a candidate for president by a people's mandate in Los Angeles. The confusion between high visibility and power is natural: our false hopes are nurtured by the deliberate invisibility of the real powers— the network heads who write Cronkite's news scripts for him, who photograph him in or near a simulated or real newsroom where the sounds of wire service machines and typewriters and telephones indicate that his desk is the center of the action wherein power and wealth and wisdom and secrets are exchanged. But Cronkite is referred to by network heads as "talent"; he is employed because he is believable.

William S. Paley, when he was head of CBS, said in a rare interview, "the believability factor is a very, very important factor. And it's a very fine line, too. If you go over that line, you get in trouble." The so-called "believability factor" is a concept peculiar to the fame age. We used to vote for honest Abe. But honesty today is too simple and direct for public consumption—it refers to essence, to risk. Now we vote for image and visibility.

President "Jimmy" Carter has that "believability factor," and he may or may not have honesty as well. His image of easygoing accessibility perplexes both the public and the press, who are accustomed to having to work hard for a glimpse of power. His apparent availability makes us all suspicious. We perceive his openness as contrived manipulation: we try to read his candor as code. But Carter is a master at both the fame and power games: he flaunts his image and keeps his power to himself.

The fame game is a visible power struggle in itself, but its power is elusive. Jacqueline Onassis may use her fame to attract the attention necessary to get New York's Grand Central Station preserved as a landmark; Anita Bryant is a good fame front for the anti-Gay Rights people; Jerry Lewis can raise money for muscular dystrophy; Marlon Brando can get media attention for American Indians; Joanne Woodward can raise contributions for ballet companies; Robert Redford can compel sympathy for ecology and raise money to produce "All The President's Men." Because we follow their fame with the nearly hysterical religious vitality that medieval virgins reserved for their heroes, their causes for a moment become our causes. But even our biggest fame winners—Jacqueline Bouvier Kennedy Onassis, Clark Gable, Joe DiMaggio, Mary Pickford, Muhammed Ali, Fred Astaire, Ed Sullivan, even Carson, Cronkite or Walters—captured together for posterity in the ultimate fame mosaic, could not keep a war from breaking out, or sway an election, or change the consciousness of the public on their own. They simply don't have the power.

What they do have is a phenomenon called *fame power*, the appearance of or access to power which, if their public believes in it, *is* a limited form of power. Mediacrats have fame power because they seem to know what's happening before the rest of us know. But Barbara Walters' version of what's happening, like her relationships with her interviewees, is not her own. It is a multi-million-dollar production, arranged and underwritten by somebody else. Still, because we think she knows more than she's telling, and because she seems to have the inside track to just about everybody else who's famous, we watch and listen to her carefully and are thus manipulated and controlled, whether she wishes it or not.

New Yorkers have fame power because they appear to know what we'll be buying before we buy it. Washington politicos have it because they seem to have access to the most powerful figures in America. Hollywood's movie stars have it because they look and act as if they know the secret to eternal popularity. Sports figures, news victims, and game show winners have it for just a split second—as long as they're center stage, and are officially part of what is happening, and are touching the lives of their countrymen while they're at it. As long as any famous person seems to have or know something that is kept just slightly beyond our reach, held back just enough to keep us hungry for more, that person has fame power. If he uses his fame to advance good causes, so much the better, but oftentimes that's not power, its fame philanthropy. On some occasions, conversely, if he uses negative fame to support evil intentions he may succeed. Recently, a man made hundreds of obscene phone calls to single women in his home town, threatening to kill them if they did not cooperate with his lewd demands. He had a high rate of cooperation because he seized attention immediately: "Don't laugh. I have a rifle trained on you. I know what I'm doing. You must obey me. I was on the news last week." He was a famous masher. His claim to fame gave him the power to make his victims jump.

Marshall McLuhan alluded to fame power when he first

wrote about the effects of television on mass culture. He proclaimed that the message—the information, the news, the secrets, the content, the interviews, the documentaries—is irrelevant, that the medium of television itself is the message. The information that television sends us is electronic and subliminal, he argued, not informative in the traditional sense of the word. Subsequent experiments and theorizing have confirmed his argument that it does not matter what we watch, it is simply *that* we watch which makes us passive and frivolous—and vulnerable to its power.

Even the *New York Times* now acknowledges that "although we used to live in a world of nature, we now live in a world of information"—meaning, of course, second-hand information, the kind of knowledge that we accept because we believe in the "believability factor" of what the opinion-makers tell us: that we live in a global village; that some disasters are more newsworthy than others; that there are *insiders*—people in the know—who have the power to do things never done before, and who have the answers to the problems which plague us. But fame power is by definition symbolic, and—if McLuhan is right—anything newscasters or opinion makers or stars or politicians proclaim to us on television is information without meaning, color without value, light and shadow without form. If the medium is indeed the message, the American fame industry's *coup de fame* is that power and fame have been rendered indistinguishable through television—making those with fame power appear mythic and immortal because television itself has the power to make exhibitionism look like heroism, insanity look like authority, hype look like genius, image look like substance, and an instant look like history.

If television provides the main forum for the fame age, its complements are *People* and *Us* and *Ear* and newspaper headlines and radio broadcasts that all feed on the television formula: quick, short, heady statements; big, lively, attention-grabbing photos; snappy, punchy, entertaining, gossipy

187

in language. Even McLuhan himself has fallen prey to the insidious era he once warned us about: "At 4 A.M.," reveals *People* magazine, "Herbert Marshall McLuhan, hip prophet of the sixties for whom 'the medium is the message,' awakens in his Toronto bedroom and slips into an ancient green bathrobe. He hurries into the kitchen not for breakfast but for a taste of biblical scholarship. For an hour he pours over scriptures in Greek, Latin, French, German and English, while gnawing on an orange." In the fame age, McLuhan's public genius is reduced to absurdity.

When there is no longer a recognizable difference between an instant and history, the profound fame that Ovid sought—classic, everlasting, mortal, mythic—is meaningless. Our short attention spans have set it aside, along with old-fashioned notions of glory and genius and honor and truth. Instead of seeking "everlasting fame" for affirmation that we exist, we seek instant celebrity, the illusion of fame. Instead of defining existence for ourselves, we wait for the news to define it for us. Instead of finding meaning in our lives, we are overwhelmed by public images which render local reputation obsolete. Images of Onassises, Kennedys, Monroes, Carters, Hearsts, and Mansons cast our fantasies, drug our imaginations, and draw us away from intimacies, re-defining our hopes and ambitions.

Everyone who has a television set or reads articles about the private lives of total strangers plays the fame game. The only way to enjoy it is to acknowledge its rules and its players and its formidable powers. But once we absorb it into our private lives, once we invest our time and energy and personal care in the behind-the-scenes activities and gossip and private affairs of the fame game players, we become nothing more than pawns of the fame game.

And, since many of us nurse an inkling that fame is worth bowing down to because it looks like a link to immortality, the dream of becoming a living legend still drives many performers and audiences to fame frenzies. Within passive dreams of meeting Farrah Fawcett or Robert Redford or appearing on a game show or a talk show or the news, is the latent, old-fashioned thrust at power that made Ovid think that fame could make him live forever. Although the fame industry has redefined the myth and the hero in show business terms, old-fashioned fame lust rears its head in small time and big time arenas all the time. Only if we insist on separating substance from image, illusion from reality, message from medium, and news from real life, can we keep the fame game and all its famous players in their proper place.

The tragic effect of the fame game is that it divests the audience of its power to discern things for itself, and gives that power to those who produce the game. But every time we turn off the set, or turn away from Walter Cronkite, or close the covers of *People* magazine, or dismiss the hype and insist upon hard information, we in the audience can reclaim our power and can still enjoy the fame game while we get on with the business of living our own lives. Otherwise, here we go: we pull up the floor pillows, lean back, flip on the set, and consume the fame that those in power feed us.

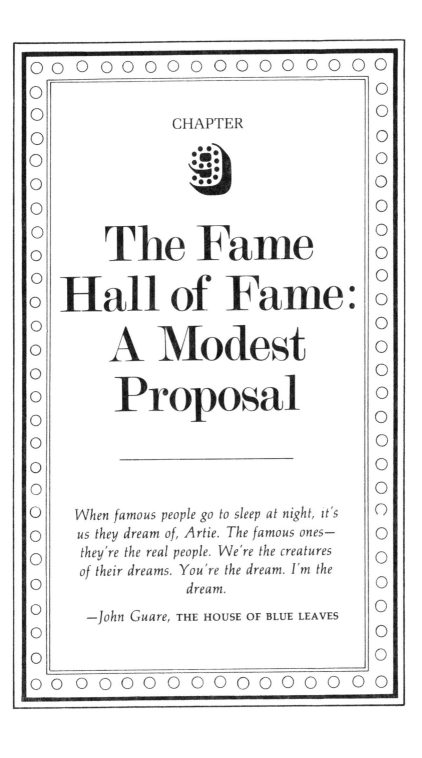

CHAPTER

9

The Fame Hall of Fame: A Modest Proposal

When famous people go to sleep at night, it's us they dream of, Artie. The famous ones— they're the real people. We're the creatures of their dreams. You're the dream. I'm the dream.

—John Guare, THE HOUSE OF BLUE LEAVES

America's official Hall of Fame stands on the campus of Bronx Community College of the City University of New York in New York City. Designed by the American architect Stanford White (who is not in it) in 1900, it is called the Hall of Fame for Great Americans and exists as a semicircular corridor of granite columns. Between the columns are 102 spaces for bronze busts of the electees, each of whom represents one of five fields: arts, sciences, humanities, government, and business and labor. Anyone wishing to nominate a person to the Hall of Fame for Great Americans must submit a proposal in writing to the executive director of the Hall's board of trustees: the candidate must have been a U.S. citizen when alive and must have been dead for twenty-five years or more. This is because fame in the official Hall of Fame cannot be enjoyed by the living; the twenty-five-year-old mantle of immortality can only be bestowed upon those already dead and thereby can raise them from the grave—not for a recap in *People* magazine but for the sake of official posterity. Thus, since entrance to the Hall of Fame is based upon past achievements rather than immediate victories in the fame game, the Hall of Fame is itself dead—no fun, no gossip, no secrets, no Sally Quinn leaks or Barbara Walters interviews or Jack Anderson scoops. No nominees to step out of limousines at exclusive premieres, or chat with Johnny Carson or flirt with Rona Barrett or cut the ribbon at the World Trade Center. They are *institutionally* immortalized and therefore beyond the fame game Americans play today, the game that is not based on achievement so much as it is on image—the game that cherishes the idea of being known for being well-known, and that allows both audience and performers to vie for that favored fame moment. No wonder the latest news we hear about the Hall of Fame is that it may soon become a "defunct institution."

Although the official Hall of Fame has no real or living pertinence for Americans in the fame age, it has produced countless spinoffs: the International College of Surgeons in Chicago honors chosen surgeons and scientists in its own Hall of Immortals. Select farmers can be found in Kansas City's Agricultural Hall of Fame, Indians in the National Hall of Fame for Famous American Indians at Andarko, Oklahoma, and Western heroes in the National Cowboy Hall of Fame in Oklahoma City. There are famous tailors and merchants in the Merchandise Mart Hall of Fame in Chicago, famous senators in the Senate Hall of Fame in Washington D.C., famous women in the Women's Hall of Fame in Seneca Falls, New York, and famous sports heroes in various halls of fame for baseball, bowling, boxing, football, golf, and tennis everywhere else.

But it is because these minor-league halls of fame follow the pattern of the big-league one, where entrance is based on achievement, that the transitory fame of its candidates, the stuff that keeps the fame game sustained in the immediate present, is denigrated by submission committees and boards of directors. They believe in institutionalized immortality and therefore rise above the fame game, making election to this or that hall of fame more esoteric than heralded, more a sign of death than eternal life, more obscure than famous. No fun.

194

What is fun about the fame game? The Academy Awards, with all its sham and posing and fake glitter and awkward moments, while it cannot possibly recapture the magic of Old Hollywood, is still fun. That's why Hollywood's stars still attend the pageant even though their contracts no longer specify that they have to; and that's why we watch it, too. So, too, in an attempt to recapture the lost magic of the Academy Awards, to exploit the tension and suspense and involvement of both the audience and the nominees, a growing number of springtime gatherings of fame-dealers, derivative of the Academy Awards, has begun to appear. In Hollywood alone there are annual ceremonies for the presentation of TV Comedy Awards, Golden Globe Awards, American Music Awards, Sci Fi Awards, People's Choice Awards, Grammy Awards, Country & Western Music Awards, Boy Scout Awards, Girl Scout Awards, Campfire Girl Awards, Four H Awards, Magic Awards, Director Awards, Writers Guild Awards, Academy Awards, and Genii Awards, to name just a few.

Nationally we have the National Academy Awards, National Bicentennial Essay Awards, National Book Awards, National Journalism Awards, National Magazine Awards, National Medal of Honor Awards, National Medicine Awards, National Miss America Awards, National Miss Teen-Age America Awards, National Miss Universe Awards, and Left-hander of the Year Awards

The ceremonies resemble one another—the suspense, the announcement, the rush of pride, the applause, the thanks. At the New York Pistol Club for Creative Gunmanship, the award presentation for killing a robber who came into a liquor store is not much different from the presentation for Best Translation at the National Book Awards.

But the key factor for making fame awards famous themselves is to sprinkle the excitement of the ceremony upon the nonfamous audience. The producers of The People's Television Awards got the right idea when they combined both the exclusivity of an awards celebration (only a few are chosen

195

as best) with the democracy of letting everybody make the choice. By giving the television audience credit for selecting our favorite performers, they also give us a sense of involvement with the fame of the winners—so the ratings for this pageant are high. Such awards are a natural extension of the older tradition of myth-sustaining rituals: when we are the Greek chorus, the priests, the powerful elite, the Great Controllers who place the blessing upon the chosen few, we become more powerful than the gods and goddesses or stars we immortalize.

So *Photoplay*, the *Ladies Home Journal*, most of the polling services now ask "average people" to tell them who are the ten most popular women or men, the best or worst dressed, the most or least powerful. Many professional groups have found it handy to exploit the mystique of fame by giving awards and simultaneously promoting a product. The Optical Manufacturers Association runs an annual "Best Dressed Eyes" survey of its members in which ten personalities are chosen for their "choice of eyewear in public appearance." In 1977 Ann-Margret won because of her "over-sized gradient-tinted rimless glasses"; runners-up were Dorothy Hamill, Warren Beatty, Robert Redford, Princess Grace of Monaco, Sophia Loren, Telly Savalas, Frank Sinatra, and Amy Carter.

All of these awards involve, exploit, profit from, and sustain the famous. But none of them focuses on the central fact that the fame game itself is a tough and competitive arena in which the American dream is constantly recycled and winners and losers are constantly rising and falling. Surely this arena—perhaps even more than all others—is worthy of an awards ceremony, perhaps even a parade, in which awards would be presented not for achievement but for manipulating images, for confusing audience with performers, for making hard work seem effortless, for converting fear of death into promise of immortality. This, then, would be the Fame Hall of Fame, acknowledging excellence

196

in the achievements of fame itself, each award for which would be named after fame's established national archtypes.

LOW-PROFILE FAME

Jacqueline Bouvier Kennedy Onassis is photographed everywhere but seems always to be hiding. She smiles for photographers in dressing rooms of opening night stars at the Palace, yet she claims she wants a low profile. When Viking Press staged a media launching to publicize a book she had edited, her boss came along to instruct journalists not to ask personal questions. Using personal fame to publicize professional but obscure work is Onassis' masterly fame mode. In fact, she brilliantly, almost effortlessly, orchestrates her own contradiction in terms. She is at once present and inaccessible. Photographed going up the escalator, Jackie and her daughter Caroline cast their eyes downward like Victorian virgins, shy and modest. A photo of Ziegfeld Follies' girls on the wall nearby presents a nice contrast to their demure presence. Onassis would never tell journalists, "I *am* the Academy Awards," like Elizabeth Taylor, or "I *am* drugs," like Salvador Dali. That is not her style, and besides, she doesn't need to.

Hers is the graceful, dignified counterpart to Frank Sinatra's bullish arrogance. Like him, she is a mythic figure, touching our past, present, and future. Her presence unites us mythically, and to see her in person is a moment of *déjà vu*.

So every glimpse of Jacqueline Onassis is an event for the glimpser, and there are photographers whose full-time job is to catch her at ease, who have earned promotions and six-figure fees for a snap of the former First Lady, former wife of one of the richest men in the world, whose achievements, like those of Dean Martin and Jimmy Carter, are rendered irrelevant by the glamour of her photographs. She belongs to us, we feel.

197

Andy Warhol emulates her passive-aggressive fame pose, but he is merely famous, not mythic. A genius of self-advertising, he flaunts his double message by appearing hours late for his own press parties. "One more flash and I'm going home," he threatens to photographers who wait for him as he steps in and out of his limousine. He is a social darling, nonthreatening and famous. Truman Capote calls him a sphinx without a secret. His albino, plain look makes him appear so utterly unaggressive that he can sometimes get the coverage of a Jacqueline Onassis. But at New York media events, his appearance is a sign of establishment, whereas Onassis' is a sign of blessedness.

PUBLIC IMAGE FAME

The public's urge to know what a famous person is *really* like is a frivolous one. Chances are most of us don't have the answer to who we ourselves really are. And public access to the privacy of a famous person is by definition a contrived one: candor is not likely from someone who knows he is being watched. What is available instead is a public statement, usually censored or composed by a publicist. The publicist is hired for that reason, like a speechwriter or a playwright: to create a *persona*, a public mask. The reasons people seek this kind of fame vary: they may be people who, like Woody Allen and Joanne Woodward, always wished they were someone else; they may be people so self-involved that, like Barbra Streisand and Jon Peters, they believe the whole world is waiting to hear their story.

That moment when a person is both consumed by his own performance and by his own perception of the performance, that is the moment of arrival, the personal *coup de fame*. If a genius, as Fitzgerald held, is a person who can hold two contradictory thoughts in his head without going crazy, so a person who can at once perform for others and observe himself performing—and enjoy it—is a fame champion.

198

In the days of Old Hollywood, publicist Jay Allen was hired to "handle" young Gene Autry. Allen invented the story that when Autry was a young teletype operator back home in Oklahoma, he happened to be singing to himself one slow night when Will Rogers walked in. "Say boy, you're good!" Rogers said, "You ought to be in pictures!" So Autry upped and quit and went out to Hollywood, and the rest is history.

Years later, Allen and his partner arranged to have the famous Autry's hometown re-named Gene Autry, Oklahoma. The day of the dedication ceremony, Allen and his partner and Autry rode in their limousine down the main street of the town. Autry turned to them and said, while pointing, "Look, there's the Western Union Office where Will Rogers walked in and discovered me." When the two partners looked at each other and laughed, Autry was offended and shouted at them, "Hey, you guys are my publicists; you mean you never heard the story of how I was discovered?"

MULTIPLE FAME

"Power is the ultimate aphrodisiac," observed Henry Kissinger when he was Secretary of State; but once his power expired, he settled for fame and seems to do just fine by it. In the same way that he juggled socialites, movie stars, and kings and shahs during his term of office, today he juggles network jobs, teaching jobs, writing contracts, dinner invitations, and smiling at photographers, and he is as full of contradictions as ever.

Warrior, diplomat, scholar, or mannequin, Kissinger always looks the same: stocky, plump, plain, knowing more than he's telling. So when Bloomingdale's opened in Washington, although it was near the end of Kissinger's reign, he was shown in *New York* magazine holding a Bloomingdale's shopping bag. The photo had been retouched: the shopping

199

bag was simply painted into a photo that had been snapped of Kissinger and aides two years earlier. Lawsuit material, but did Kissinger sue? Of course not. He knew that he was the subject of the photograph and that Bloomingdale's made him look chic.

Unless stars have to select their endorsements carefully, they'll lose their power to sell by fame by association. According to *More* magazine, "Robert Mitchum agrees to a public-service pitch for the Job Corps; for a million bucks Steve McQueen agrees to pitch for Suzuki—but only in Japan. And, occasionally, a staggering news bulletin shakes the industry: John Wayne, the Duke, sells out to Datril for a mere $400,000.

"When it works, the celeb strategy pays off in spades. Karl Malden (crowned *Ad Age's* 'Presenter of the Year') has proved a bonanza for American Express. So has O.J. Simpson, crashing through airport crowds in a mad rush for his Hertz. The success of such campaigns is invariably attributed to the inspired 'hook' or logical 'connect' between the celeb and the product."

The implication is always that a famous person is still, privately, a common man; he's just like you and me. Besides, he's just like Rockefeller if he has American Express and Diner's Club and Master Charge—he can buy anything Rockefeller can, and so can we. Plus he's got fame, so if we wear a tee-shirt with his picture on it, or shave with the same razor he uses, we reverse the axiom: we make the common man—us—a famous person.

It's a triumph for both performer and audience, this false equation. And like Jack Nicholson, the plain, shy Telly Savalas adores being adored for being One Of The Guys, for fitting in, for being popular. He is popular for being popular, but no one sees how hard he works to create the effect, since part of his achievement is the image of effortlessness.

Gillette commercials began with *look sharp, feel sharp, be sharp* to the tune of a boxing bell ringing. Now they're more sophisticated: we see fame's Telly Savalas looking in the mirror in such a way that we look in the mirror and Telly's image comes back at us.

Savalas' nickname is usefully ambiguous too. He is "Telly," Mr. Television; not handsome but not threatening either, in spite of Kojak's bad temper and the violence of his program, because he is rendered smaller than we are by the tube. Gillette understands the power of fame and the power of television promotion. Rather than sponsoring an award for the greatest blade of the year and giving it to themselves the way other promoters do, Gillette chooses to sponsor the All-Star Baseball Game. They prefer fame by association. It works to sell blades, in spite of the fact that they lose money on the All-Star game, and their ad works to sustain the fame game, too. If Savalas can shave his head without cutting himself, he must be a real man, and if we can look like that and feel that way about ourselves and borrow Savalas' image for a while, so much the better.

Similar campaigns have been staged by Johnny Carson Clothiers, by Candice Bergen's CIE cologne, in which she says "CIE IS ME," implying that if we use it, we can use her. The advertisers exploit the confusion of customer and hawker, knowing we want to be like that famous person. So Robert Young of Marcus Welby fame can get on TV looking exactly like the doctor he portrays, explain to the audience in the Welby bedside manner that many people think he is a doctor even though he isn't, and then launch into a spiel for Sanka, convincing us that if Doctor Welby drinks it, it must be healthy.

PIGGYBACK FAME

Diane von Furstenberg inventively established her fame as a socialite by marrying the Austrian Prince Egon von Furstenberg and "going everywhere with him," as she says, "even to the opening of a toothpaste factory." Once she even

201

arranged to give birth to her child three weeks early by Caesarean section, so that she would be healed in time to attend a fashion show for a dress business that became so successful and so famous that it established a new trend in the local fame game. Suddenly socialites Charlotte Ford, C.Z. Guest, and Mary McFadden were following suit by pushing their labels for the Seventh Avenue fashion industry, which capitalizes on the insecurity that makes consumers want to wear the labels and monograms of famous strangers. And then Prince Egon hoisted himself up by her bootstraps and gave *his* name to a line of menswear, and following on *his* footsteps was the grandson of Sir Winston Churchill. So this now separated couple has lived nicely off each other's reputation, and the fantasy of their coming together to visit the children and to sign contracts rivals the titillating appeal of other famous ex-couples: Sonny and Cher, Burton and Taylor, Andy Williams and Claudine Longet.

Prince Egon claims his nobility means nothing to him, that he enjoys taking buses just like everybody else.

"I'm lucky," he says. "All the powerful people in America are accessible to me. Not just because of my title. When your family owns Fiat Motor Company with 350,000 workers, it's like being a government within a government. I was brought up with their kids, I went to school, I lived with those people from when I am one. They don't want to have outsiders." By soft-pedalling his royal privilege, Egon von Furstenberg imitates the American democratic fame mode, but the mystique of his royalty still gives him status with which he can sell clothes, and entrance into the places he *really* wants to go. The true nobility in America, he says, are "really like the very WASP Long Island people. They always mix together and never really get out, and Diane met them because she married me. There are only two or three ways of getting in. Either you're very, very successful in business so you have a power base, 30 million dollars and up, or you marry somebody in it. A Billy Baldwin will get into it. But Elizabeth Taylor or someone very, very famous would not even be invited as an ornament because she would bring in reporters and photographers."

In the past, even in old fashioned towns like Washington, social prominence was more of a drawing card than wide visibility. But in New York, high society is just another statusphere which insures the social elite a place in the New York fame tableau.

BAD TASTE FAME

A barber who gives a shave and a haircut to a famous person feels as though he holds that famous person in his hands: he senses what his customer is *really* like as he brings the razor to his cheek and the scissors to his scalp. Afterwards the star takes the shave and the haircut to important places—to bed, up on stage, to inner sanctums. The barber feels a special intimacy, a privilege, an involvement. The manicurist comes home and reports to her husband, "I did Liza Minnelli today," and feels special.

If you once rode on an elevator with Judy Garland, twenty years later you would still feel involved somehow in her life and death because you were close to her once, you occupied the same space, you had even been near enough to kiss her or kill her if you'd chosen. It's that existential sense of sharing the same oxygen, of having a (not as false as one might wish) sense of power over the person's destiny, of being in the presence of an immortal, that leads to a lifelong involvement in a famous life.

The personal physician has an actual life-and-death relationship with his famous patient, so when the public seeks information about the personal life of a famous figure, the doctor is a handy source. Marilyn Monroe's psychiatrist was courted as an important link to her legend after her suicide. Xaviera Hollander's gynecologist's practice doubled after she named him in her book, *The Happy Hooker.* Woody Allen's analyst is consulted by hopeful comedians.

Some years before Pope Pius XII ascended the papal throne, he contacted Italian ophthalmologist Dr. Bernardo Galeazzi-Lisi for treatment of a minor eye infection. Their relationship continued throughout Pope Pius' rule, and when the Pope became fatally ill, Dr. Galeazzi-Lisi was there to take charge as his physician and alleviate the suffering as best he could. One of his first acts was to arrange for a professional photographer to take pictures of the dying Pope attempting to do push-ups and receiving enemas; his apparent motive for this was to perform a service to the millions of people who were interested in seeing the dying Pope up close, and to hear the true behind-the-scenes story of how difficult and painful and agonizing the death was. According to *Time* magazine, after the Pope died Dr. Galeazzi-Lisi contacted magazines all over the world and solicited bids on his photographs and death bed journal. "The price list: $13,320 for an anecdotal article on his life with the Pope to include clinical details; $8,000—later reduced to $3,200—for an hour-by-hour account of the Papal agony; $3,200 for photographs of the death throes; $1,600 for a story on the embalming process."

Of course the bad taste of Dr. Galeazzi-Lisi, while extreme, is nothing new in the fame game arena, where many people exploit their relationships and private associations and sometimes painful experiences for the sake of becoming well-known. Barbara Howar, by describing her conversation with Jackie Kennedy about shaving hair off their legs, displayed the kind of allusion to intimacy that built her career.

Just because people aren't at center stage doesn't mean they're not as ambitious as their clients, or that they're passive. Agent Sue Mengers, for example, is hardly passive—in fact she is even more famous than some of her clients. So it is natural for the associates, friends, and underlings—those who feed and support the fame of others—to feel a resentment for the people who *are* center stage. When that resentment is not held in check, the people behind the scenes become the ones who secret-monger and leak classified information. The private secretary writes the biography, the chef the personal cookbook, the mistress the exposé, and the dog-keeper, doorman, chauffeur and valet all get into the act. Sometimes their works are endearing portraits of the famous people they once served, while at other times they are back-biting tracts, but all are vehicles by which these lesser mortals may become famous themselves. Of course, when people like Galeazzi-Lisi realize that the simple I-knew-him-when role doesn't always bring fame by association, they sometimes stoop to the grotesque.

But in spite of public disgust at his exploitation of the Pope's death, Galeazzi-Lisi won anyway: for unlike Howar, or the chauffeur or mistress or dog-keeper—all of whom feel they have high cause for exhibiting bad taste—Galeazzi-Lisi became famous by his bad taste *alone,* for without it, he never would have gotten his photograph in *Time* magazine, and never would have invaded the consciousness of millions.

WINNING FAME

People who are famous in one category or arena often covet fame in another. Very powerful industrialists would love to run a country; many doctors would love to be businessmen; fashion designers would like to be architects; television stars would like to be movie stars; athletes would like to be big businessmen. They flirt competitively with each other's fame. And the truth is that many people do move from one field to another, they do succeed in more than one arena, indicating that their quest is more than for achievement in a given field: the quest, like Ovid's, is "that I may be celebrated throughout the whole earth."

Muhammed Ali is a famous champion who wins, not only

against the brute force of the heaviest heavyweights of the world, but also against the wrath of his original fans and promoters. After he changed his name from Cassius Clay, after he became a Muslim and refused to go to war, Ali was ostracized from the statusphere of boxing. He could have disappeared then, but it was his monumental fame that kept him alive in boxing, fame that in part got him reinstated: the fans wouldn't let him go. Although he never had the power to control the arena or run the show, Ali won those rounds and many others because he masterfully projected an image that beat them all in the ring and won the hearts of the nonboxing public as well.

But in order to live on as a living legend, Ali will soon slip from the fame slot of boxer into the full-time image of a champion and substitute a sense of championship for his true gift. Sparring with Sylvester Stallone at the Academy Awards podium, he trumpets his own transition from the arena of boxing to that of show business. But Ali began setting up his eclectic fame long ago. Poet, religious spokesman, world heavyweight champion, he calls himself "the onliest person that can speak to everybody in the whole world."

And he can. At a lunch with the fragile, nonviolent, famous poet Marianne Moore, he charmed her and their host, George Plimpton, and even got Moore to help him write a poem about her. While the bragging pronouncements of other famous people—such as the Beatles' statement that "We're more popular than Jesus"—get them in trouble, Ali has paid his dues. He gets us to enjoy his fame pleasures with him. "It's just a job," he grins. "Grass grows, birds fly, waves pound the sand. I beat people up."

And we love him for it. Other celebrities have trouble pleasing the very crowd that makes them famous. Writer Erica Jong tries desperately to have sympathy and fame at the same time, but she doesn't get it. We don't want to hear about the hardships of her fame and fortune. The Fonz tried calling himself Henry Winkler and writing in *Newsweek* about how lonely it is at the top. We ignored Winkler and kept loving the Fonz. Fame whining is not an effective fame pose. Not until a Monroe or a Prinze actually destroys himself to really put an end to the business of the show are we convinced that fame is unpleasant. It is not the particular success we're interested in in many cases, but that element of fame that makes a person seem chosen, special, saved. So to play down fame's pleasure, like a Paul Newman, can be charming. To complain about it is offensive. But laughing and enjoying it—in the Ali mode—is winning.

NEGATIVE FAME

Sometimes crime can be a shortcut to fame. Claudine Longet, wife of famous singer Andy Williams, famous friend of the famous Kennedys, upstaged her husband by shooting her lover, Spider Savitch, just as Sara Jane Moore upstaged President Ford's visit to San Francisco.

Public villain Charles Manson, certainly famous, was a star to the members of his tribe. It may be argued by some that he was a leader, and by others that he was a priest. But what is certain is that the fame game has touched him as surely as it touched the huge audiences for both book and movie "Helter Skelter," and the millions who will never forget Manson's seemingly satanic visage peering out at them from the front page of their paper.

By causing a crisis that was bankable, like Entebbe and the Hindenberg disaster, Manson became bankable himself. Furthermore, his crimes involved famous people who became more famous after he had ruined and/or ended their lives. It was possible to confuse Sharon Tate with other Hollywood beauties before her murder. Her marriage to Polanski gave her some additional fame by association, but Manson made sure she would be a legend, albeit not in her own time.

207

Now helicopter maps to stars' homes include a diagram of her house, and although it is the wrong house, people living in the one which is mis-marked are constantly being bothered by low-flying helicopters carrying paying guests who are anxious to visit that scene of the crime.

The *Helter Skelter* book sold millions and the televised version, even on re-run, broke all records for viewers. Now Charles Manson has made recordings of his songs and is trying to market them from jail. His followers still follow him and their trials make headlines.

His is perhaps the most violent and interesting crime since the Leopold and Loeb murder of Bobby Frank, celebrated in *Compulsion*. He has made a vicious crime, if not pay, at least make him famous.

Although there are vast differences between a star and a hero and a leader and a villain and a priest, the fame industry obscures those differences by giving everyone equal attention. So Manson will live on, long after the real horror of his deed has passed, when future generations will regard him as a famous person of a bygone era.

SURVIVAL FAME

Memoirs are the traditional way of permanently cleaning up one's personal act; but television has presented the opportunity for doing it instantly. So Richard Nixon, for an estimated half-million-dollar benefit to himself, agreed to let David Frost interview him on television the first time he appeared publicly after his disgrace and fall from power. The appearances were carefully rehearsed—Nixon with his staff and Frost with his before the interviews took place; and they were agreed-to beforehand by extensive contracts which did not specifically outline what questions would be asked, or in what order. It sounded at first like a history-making exchange in which the fallen president would "tell all"—or at least be forced to answer questions about the parts he didn't want to tell.

Nixon's accomplishment—substituting a round of the fame game for the judiciary procedure—was considerable. None of his remarks were stated under oath, none of them challenged by a judge or jury; only mediacrat Frost was there with his clipboard and the press to respond or countercharge or discuss or question. So Richard Nixon vaulted over the heads of jurors, judge, prosecutors, and the American people, and went directly to history. Not only did the televised fame game make money and history for him in itself, it also got simultaneous coverage in *Time* and *Newsweek* and every front page in the country. And it gave Nixon a new kind of credibility that he shared with the Fonz when he publicly complains about the loneliness of fame, or Raquel Welch when she whines about her psychoanalysis to TV mediacrat Rona Barrett, or with Don Rickles when he names and insults his enemies on television. Why, Nixon seemed to ask, should he settle for the old kind of justice when there is this new fame mode? After all, just because he had been president, should he be deprived of celebrity? Isn't it a free country? A democracy? And as, one by one, Nixon obliterated the moral issues of the Watergate scandal, he established once and for all the irrelevance of morality, honor, heroism, justice, good will—flaunting fame as democracy pushed to the absurd.

To be sure, he had the help of David Frost, whom America first met via television in "That Was The Week That Was," a satirical review in which he blended news with television skits. We had watched Frost publicly court Diahann Carroll, we had seen him scold Adam Clayton Powell, we had even viewed him moderating an underwater kissing contest. All of this had paved the way for the Nixon interviews, his ultimate news vaudeville act.

It was no surprise, then, that Frost could moderate this television fame spectacular, undercutting special prosecutors, beating out even Woodward and Bernstein; and after each televised "interview" the newspaper headlines never mentioned Nixon's tone (maudlin, self-pitying) or recalled the style of the Checkers speech (self-righteous, whining) but remained literal, factual, linear, and therefore portentiously important: "Nixon says he is sorry, he let the American people down."

Having set the stage for himself, Nixon was able to redefine the terms of his confession even as he misrepresented the facts by saying, "I impeached myself." Still, historians will quote what he says he has done. His fame slot as president has given him that direct access to history whether he deserved it or not. So in spite of declining ratings in his declining years, Nixon has accomplished the ultimate *coup de fame* by drawing on the infinite possibilities of the fame age. If his claim to power or morality is dubious, his claim to fame is undeniable. If he is blurring the American dream into something shallow and simplistic and transitory and cheap, he is also making it come true.

Of course the Fame Hall of Fame, regardless of how many other categories it might honor or how many spaces for bronze busts it might have, would still be a hall of strangers: these are not people we really know, not people we run into down the block or invite over for coffee or vote for in local elections. These are still images to us, no matter how close we feel to them and how much they invade our dreams or waking consciousness. Why settle for celebrating famous strangers? Why not nurture a personal sense of fame power instead of that nagging sense of irrelevance that comes with a permanent seat in the audience? Why not honor fame ourselves, right there in each city or neighborhood or block, by celebrating a local Fame Day, say on the first day of May every year, and inviting everybody to delineate fame on a local scale? After all, anybody can make lists and vote for any ten bests he or she likes and give awards. A famous family has already done just that by publishing a book of lists, ranging from "the fifty worst films of all time" to "the twelve greatest Jews of all time." But if we did it, we wouldn't have to be quite so grandiose, we could simply look around us and separate those whose fame has meaning to us from those whose lives are still obscure. We could then each gain control over that confusing tension, that sense of blessedness of being in the presense of an immortal. For if we chose the fame winners every year, we would control the fame game and control its impact on our lives.

So on Fame Day local arenas all over America would select a yearly list of favorite fame figures. Flowers could be thrown, autographs given, pictures taken of local fans posing with local winners. The celebration would involve everyone and would be taken personally rather than electronically or nationally or generically or institutionally. The local gossip columnists would not have to write about strangers: instead of gossip about Woody Allen's distant New Year's Eve party, where distant if famous basketball stars from the Knicks, or dancers like Nureyev, or writers, actors, politicians, or other nationally known figures were seen, so that the reader's imagination boggles at the fame fantasy of standing in the room with all these remote strangers, our fame machine would feed us images as well as the flesh-and-blood reality of friends and neighbors, helping us recapture some of the lost magic of old-fashioned fame.

We would have to be careful, though, for this notion of tightening the fame circle and spreading fame to local participants has already been tried and has already failed. In the spring of 1973, in Washington D.C., the Kennedy family, instead of hosting a conventional masked charity ball, collaborated with other fame powers for a benefit for their charity for the mentally retarded. The producers of "Funny Lady" agreed to hold the film's premiere at the Kennedy Center. The world heavyweight champion of the world, Muhammed Ali, agreed to come. The press release contained more living legends than had appeared under one roof since

211

President Kennedy's fortieth birthday party when Marilyn Monroe sang "Happy Birthday."

Barbra Streisand sang in the great hall for President Ford; senators, millionaires, mediacrats like Barbara Walters and Dick Cavett jousted with athletes and with some specially chosen mentally retarded children. All for national television. It should have been a spectacle even greater than the Academy Awards. It had all the elements: winners, losers, face-famous, name-famous, grotesques, powers, glamour people.

The sports figures, politicians, movie stars, and socialites outdid each other and the mediacrats at fame-gawking at one another. But there was no one there who was a full-time member of the audience. *Everybody* was famous. Even the retarded children were included in the act, competing with O.J. Simpson and Barbara Walters in athletic stunts. As a charity event, it was a great success. But as a fame pageant, it was a case of overkill. When the retarded children were given center stage, the self-consciousness of the full-time co-stars like Streisand and Cavett pervaded the atmosphere. That's the risk when fame goes *too* public and forgets how important the audience really is

But we wouldn't forget; every year when Fame Day came around, we would make sure there would be a certain number of performers and a certain number of observers. We would carefully orchestrate the ceremony and devote the entire day to celebrating fame. We would establish once and for all our own fame roles and those of our townspeople. We would finally get all that awe and contempt out of our systems and get back to our own lives.

CHAPTER NOTES

CHAPTER ONE: The audience reaction to Liza Minnelli at the sneak preview of "New York,New York" was described by Joseph Torchia in the *San Francisco Chronicle* on June 6, 1977. Studs Terkel's observations about fame are taken from his review of *Celebrity Register* in *The Nation*, February 23, 1974. The Keele University poll, first reported in *New Society*, was described by Pat Horn in the July 1975 issue of *Psychology Today*. And Parson Weems' letter about George Washington appears in *Mason Locke Weems: His Works and Ways*, Emily E. Ford Skeel, editor, published by AMS Press, New York, 1976.

CHAPTER TWO: James Brady's reference to Greta Garbo and *Women's Wear Daily* appears in his book, *Superchic*, published by Little, Brown and Company, 1974.

CHAPTER THREE: Quotes by Johnny Carson used in this chapter are from Lynn Van Matre's article, "A Monologue Without Makeup: Johnny Carson," in the *Chicago Tribune*, June 6, 1976; and "Playboy Interview: Johnny Carson," *Playboy*, December 1967.

CHAPTER FOUR: Barbara Howar's description of dancing with Lyndon Johnson appears in *Laughing All The Way*, published in 1973 by Stein and Day. Doris Kearns' explanation of Johnson's attitude toward the press is from *Lyndon Johnson And The American Dream*, published by Harper and Row in 1976.

CHAPTER FIVE: Joanne Woodward's comments about being married to a star are from an interview by Mary-Lou Weisman in

Newsweek's international edition, October 7, 1974. Robert Redford's comments are from "Playboy Interview: Robert Redford," *Playboy*, December 1974. The quote by Al Pacino appears in *Off Camera* by Leonard Probst, published by Stein and Day in 1976. Barbara Howar's description of her talk with Jacqueline Kennedy appears in *Laughing All The Way*. George C. Scott's comments about fame appeared in Barbara Gelb's article, "Great Scott!" in the *New York Times Magazine*, January 23, 1977. And the Saul Bellow quote is from *Humboldt's Gift*, published by Viking Press in 1975.

CHAPTER SEVEN: Robert Evans' "only Hollywood lives" contention was quoted by Bernard Drew in an article entitled "The Man With The Golden Touch" in the November 1976 issue of *American Film*. Director Frank Pierson's description of filming "A Star Is Born" is taken from his *New West* article, "My Battles With Barbra and Jon," November 22, 1976. Producer Dino De Laurentiis' comments about the public's reaction to his movie are from "Here Comes King King," in *Time*, October 25, 1976. Both quotes by Sue Mengers are from "Dialogue on Film: Sue Mengers," *American Film*, November 1976.

CHAPTER EIGHT: William S. Paley's comment about the "believability factor" appeared in an article by Donald West entitled "The House That Paley Built —And Keeps" in the *New York Times*, October 24, 1976.

CHAPTER NINE: The quote about stars endorsing products appeared in "Madison Avenue Catches the Fallen Stars," by Jonathan Black in the May 1977 issue of *More* magazine. The description of Dr. Galeazzi-Lisi's prices for photographs of the dying Pope appeared in *Time*, November 3, 1958. And Muhammed Ali's "I beat people up" reference appeared in an interview with Joyce Maynard entitled "Life With Ali (In A Neutral Corner)" in the *New York Times*, April 6, 1977.